THE HIPPIE HITCHHIKER
FROM NEBRASKA

The Hippie Hitchhiker from Nebraska

Randy Rhody

PART I

NEBRASKA

CHAPTER 1

I was sixteen the summer I paid twenty-five dollars for a derelict '53 Chevy convertible with a dicey automatic transmission and torn vinyl seats. Eleven years old and already winter road-salt had rusted away pieces of the floor, affording glimpses of the pavement slipping by below. I bought the car with money I saved working at the Lincoln Air Force Base commissary after school and weekends, one of several boys bagging and loading groceries for tips.

As soon as I was able to drive into Lincoln, I found better work delivering chicken dinners and pizzas. It paid a minimum wage and on top of that I still got tips. The business had a fleet of four International Scouts that we drove and in no time I got the hang of the clutch and stick shift. Soon I was learning all the streets and neighborhoods in Lincoln. My view until then had been limited to riding the school bus from the base to Lincoln High School and back. There was a wider world out there and it felt pretty cool getting paid to explore it.

On the streets, I sometimes noticed two guys on motorcycles. Always the same two. There'd be a brief impression of sunglasses and old aviator goggles as they came toward me and we passed going opposite directions. Their hair was just long enough to whip around in the wind, or one might have a pirate bandana wrapped on his head. There weren't any biker gangs on the streets and these guys didn't wear club jackets of any kind. They flew by with a gypsy flamboyance, an elan that looked out of place in Lincoln, the way I felt out of place.

I wasn't actually from Nebraska. I wasn't actually from anywhere. I was born near San Francisco, but wasn't there long enough to remember. My dad was career Air Force and the military made migrants of us, more rootless than nomads. During our mobile existence we lived in a trailer court, a whistle-stop hamlet, a suburb or two, and a college town. Worst of all were the monotonous military-base apartments we sometimes occupied, where the same vomit-inspired yellow paint covered every building in sight.

Ten moves in fourteen years brought us to Lincoln Air Force Base in time for me to finish ninth grade and begin high school. Nebraska was so remote that I checked a map to be certain where it was— stranded dead center in the middle of the continent, as far from either coast as you could get. They even called themselves the Cornhusker State. To me it sounded like the Bib Overall and Long Underwear State.

No cornfield living for us though. When we arrived the military installed us in government-issue housing, a soul-draining, treeless expanse of identical one-story duplexes lined up in close-order formation. The ambient scream of fighter jets and thunder of military transports and bombers assaulted us day and night.

Lincoln High had 2,400 students divided among sophomores, juniors, and seniors. Freshmen went to the junior high. As a newcomer I was no student body notable. Those were town kids who all had long-established reputations and alliances since first grade. If ever we'd stayed in one place I might have been one of those prominent kids instead of a nonentity. I seemed to make friends easily, but early on I learned that frequent transplants came with consequences. By high school us air base kids had endured a lifelong procession of friends and classmates abruptly moving away, never to be seen again.

"Easy come, easy go," we bravely said, though each loss was like a death. Just as often we ourselves would be the dear departed. I couldn't imagine growing up with the same friends, or knowing them later as adults.

By third grade I was in my fifth school, where for some reason our class voted me king of the upcoming Valentine's Day party. I wasn't sure why they chose me. In the principal's office later, a kindly gray-haired man in wire-rimmed glasses showed me an announcement to bring home. "That's you," he said, smiling and pointing to a cartoon face of a boy wearing a crown. To be truthful, the prospect of being the center of attention was somewhat worrisome.

"We won't be here," was my mom's matter-of-fact comment when I gave her the note from school. It wasn't like her to regard me as Valentine material anyway, or to hug me proudly. I didn't have parties at home. Throughout childhood my friends weren't even allowed in the house. Making me feel wanted or special wasn't in her character. She explained we were moving again. It was the military's doing. We had our marching orders.

I was a little relieved, knowing I didn't deserve the honor. The runner-up took my place. People like him, who never moved away from friends, would go on to be prom kings and class presidents. On Valentine's Day we were in our car driving to another state, where at school number six I could look forward once again to being the new kid, a complete unknown.

Besides the after-school jobs, I labored over high school homework. I gradually earned recognition with good grades, and sometimes made the semester honor roll. Honor students stood on stage during school assemblies to receive certificates. Our names appeared in the school paper, elevating our stature among teachers and classmates.

English Literature was one of my favorite subjects. I was hypno-tized by words. I dreamed of being an acclaimed writer, someone of timeless eminence who wrote things that would become required reading for high school and college students in the future. A writer wasn't fixed to any one location, but his work and his voice were permanent.

Even though poetry wasn't part of everyday life, not like movies or sports, our teachers beguiled me into believing it was a worthwhile thing to put my mind to. I wanted to write poetry as meaningful as "quoth the raven, nevermore" or "the women come and go talking of Michelangelo." I wrote every day in order to keep in practice and form a habit of writing but I was too young to have acquired any wisdom. Most of it was scribbled gibberish, cryptic attempts to express an unformed thought, or playful combinations of unrelated words that were interesting to read or hear. Even "Randy Rhody" sounded like a poem. Or at least a nursery rhyme.

My writing would not be a lovesick tribute or social commentary. Rather it would be an unblinking glimpse into the void, the mystic work of a seer. I strived to reach a transcendent plane that wasn't grounded in everyday reality. I imagined that the greatest verses of all time had likely not been spoken or written. No doubt some Stone Age shaman had once beheld wondrous visions and never written a word. Had seen the dark matter of the universe and kept its secret.

One of my poems speculated that people who did not write or know how to write, or who lived in places where writing was unknown, may have had humankind's most exceptional and original insights and never expressed them. It began:

> *The pity of the world*
> *Is that the thoughts of an illiterate poet*
> *Must go the way*
> *   Of smoke and shade...*

Everything after "smoke and shade" consisted of awkward analogies that wandered from the initial thought, although the poetry of more accomplished writers of the era could be just as bad. I called the poem "Atlantis Revisited," thinking that the lost unwritten words of an illiterate poet were like a lost civilization.

Living out on the American Great Plains of Nebraska, remote from cultural connections, it didn't cross my mind that elsewhere in the country other young poets like me were experimenting with words. I felt like one of a kind, not part of something bigger, sort of like the two motorcyclists I sometimes saw.

Some famous authors had gotten their start on newspapers, I heard, so I signed up for journalism. One of our practice assignments was to write an interview, which gave me an excuse to meet a famous writer in person. Karl Shapiro was with the faculty at the University of Nebraska in Lincoln. His poetry had been awarded the Pulitzer twenty years earlier and we read some of his poems in English Lit, including one about a car wreck. I found his number in the Lincoln directory and telephoned to explain about the assignment. He agreed and we made an appointment. I could do stuff like that now that I had the car.

I was impressed that a great god of letters would grant time to speak to me in person, and in his own home. Karl Shapiro was in his fifties. I half expected that he'd look artsy or unconventional like a poet might look, maybe in sandals and a sweatshirt. At his door he looked domestic and well fed, with wavy white hair and black-framed glasses, in a print cotton sport shirt and khakis. You could picture him trimming the hedge or taking out the trash. His demeanor was casual and friendly.

To break the ice I said, "I met your daughter Kathy when we were in the same art appreciation class." She was a couple years older. I didn't mention that she was learning French and had taught a few of us to say *Voulez-vous coucher avec moi.*

I was too young for a give-and-take discussion. This was straight-out scripted Q and A. I read him my prepared list of unremarkable questions and took dutiful notes of his answers.

"When did you begin writing?"

"Did you always want to write poetry?"

"How did you first get published?"

In answer to one of my questions Karl admitted that at times he felt some misgivings about things he had published. I didn't ask him to elaborate, but later, having written some of the rubbish I did, I remembered his words and thought I understood. Luckily for me most of my poetry was never published, or what was published was lost. After my graded interview was returned to me marked with an A, I mailed it to him with a thank-you note.

In my senior year I dropped by Barbara Van Zandt's house to leave her something we were working on in journalism. A girl I didn't know opened the screen door part way, and I thought I recognized her. She had dark Latin eyes.

"Is Barbara here?"

"No. Everyone's out but they'll be back soon," she said with an accent.

"Hey, aren't you the exchange student at Lincoln High?" I asked.

"Yes," she said, smiling. The Van Zandts were her American host family.

"Nice meeting you. I'm Randy. What's your name?"

"Isabel, but I go by Cachito."

"You're from South America, aren't you?"

"Yes. Peru."

"Wow. Peru." I began speaking to her in my fourth-year Spanish. "*Le gustan usted los estados unidos?*" I loved Spanish. The language was a window to a completely different culture, exotic and magical, more easy-going than life as I knew it in the USA. I'd long thought that I'd like to live in Latin America some day. Peru seemed like another planet. Land of the Inca.

She stepped out onto the porch while we chatted in mangled Spanish and English. The Van Zandts arrived and invited me in for lemonade at the kitchen table. It came out that Barbara was going to a movie with her boyfriend that evening and Mrs. Van Zandt mentioned that they could take Cachito and me along. Cachito didn't really circulate except for organized school activities or with the Van Zandts. Being an exchange student, she was as much an outsider as I had been when I first came to Lincoln. Barbara looked at Cachito. Cachito and I glanced at each other. We all agreed, as much out of politeness as anything. I had just started going out with someone else, but it would be interesting to go out with the girl from Peru.

I came back later and we all went to the drive-in movie. I took her to more movies. Pretty soon she was my steady girlfriend. Every day was Valentine's Day. She smoked Kent cigarettes and I took up smoking too. On weekends we went to the football games and dances in my Chevy and cruised the streets and drive-ins afterwards like everyone else. No foreign exchange student was ever so immersed in American high school culture.

By seventeen I'd assembled a pretty normal teenage existence thanks to the Chevy. Normal except for my parents, that is. My activities at work and school, my interests in writing and girlfriends weren't buoyed by kindly nurture.

"When you turn eighteen, you're on your own." My old man had recited this fatherly precept often during my teenage years. Behind the facade they presented to others, life in their house was obedience to rules, where food, clothing, and shelter were provided as if in accord with wartime conventions for prisoners.

Patrolling the city streets in all weather and all seasons was an unaccustomed freedom. It was a relief to have some distance between me and my parents. I couldn't wait to leave for good, but as long as I was a minor it was their lawful responsibility to tolerate my existence, and vice versa.

I wasn't willing to confide in them about things that mattered to me for fear they would further stifle my dreams. I kept Cachito's existence secret from them. The emotional connection to her was unlike anything I'd known in our sterile household.

On a Sunday when I'd spent the afternoon in Lincoln with

Cachito and friends I told her I'd see her again later and drove home to check in.

"I'm going back into town," I announced after supper. On long-standing general principles, and not knowing about my date, they forbade me to leave the house.

"No. You stay home now for the rest of the day," my mom said.

"What for?"

"It's a school night." As if my grades were in jeopardy.

"So what. It's not even six o'clock." Still daylight. They hated it when I was logical.

"You do what you're told and none of your lip," my dad commanded.

"I'm not sitting around this dumb place. My friends are expecting me."

My mom was resolute. "You're not going out."

I'd suffocated enough from a lifetime of arbitrary injustices. I had built a separate existence in Lincoln of work, school, friends, and freedom.

"That's what you think," I said. I blasted out the door in a fury and never went back.

After school on Monday I looked in the newspaper classifieds and found a sleeping room eight blocks from the state capitol building, where an elderly widow named Mrs. Lohmeier rented out her three upstairs bedrooms to single working men. At seventeen, I was on my own. And just as well. Within a few weeks the Air Force transferred my family again.

CHAPTER 2

I've wondered if the rift with my parents had its origins in the UFO crash at Roswell, New Mexico a few weeks before I was born. While I learned to crawl and walk, America began producing movies that imagined first encounters with alien beings, ranging from the benevolent *The Day the Earth Stood Still* to the sinister *The Thing From Another World*. I didn't see movies or read newspapers, but my impressionable mind sensed inklings of the general hysteria in the air.

When I was four, UFOs were seen over Washington D.C. by pilots and control tower operators. We lived in Alaska that year, where an occasional moose would wander into our yard. I liked to open the front door if someone knocked, despite admonitions not to. So why didn't they put a latch on it out of my reach? One evening there was a tapping but I practiced self-restraint and remained where I was. Nevertheless, my mom told me "See who it is," and I went to the door, stepping into the early dark to welcome a visitor, and—Whoa!

An alien confronted me. In the shadowy twilight was a hulking bug-eyed creature, snuffling and snorting into my face through a dangling snout. Clearly it was no Alaskan moose, nor a wolf or a bear. It could only be a monstrosity from a flying saucer. I yelped and backed into the room, while the creature rose erect from a crouch and entered. I stood paralyzed, knowing that in moments our entire family would be obliterated from the earth and nothing I could do would prevent it.

Then puzzled, I recognized the towering figure of my dad in his Air Force khakis, removing some sort of mask. Seeing my tears, he may have regretted his scheme to teach me a lesson because he promptly sat beside me on the sofa to show it was only a gas mask. I touched the glass goggles and rubbery breathing hose and comprehended that it was an ordinary piece of military equipment.

Far from being comforted, at that moment an oozing sensation trickled from my head down my spine as I realized something more frightening than the mere presence of a space alien. The people I had total belief in had collaborated to trick and betray me, though I was unable to express as much in four-year-old words. I realized I was alone in the world. My wails escalated from terror to profound bereavement, as at the death of loved ones.

After my family left Nebraska I finished high school and traded letters with them out of a sense of duty. That's what families were supposed to do, wasn't it? At graduation I wrote to them about a handful of scholastic awards that I received, still seeking some approval that never materialized.

> One for a high national exam score, one for being a Regents Alternate, one for being designated a University of Nebraska Honor Student (gee there were only about a dozen of those), and the other is for making the Society for Academic Achievement... the high school counterpart of Phi Beta Kappa... less people made that than the Honor Society.

In my room, which I paid for out of my delivery income, I examined the paper awards with bewilderment. Were they meant to inspire self-esteem? A sense of accomplishment? They left me feeling empty and abandoned. They were deceitful. Nobody from those academic and civic organizations was going to come knocking on my door and no former teachers looked me up to offer congratulations. It was kind of depressing.

I foolishly hoped all those recognitions might encourage the old man to come up with some college money, but I was mistaken there. "If you want to go to college I'll pay your rent, but you have to pay for everything else yourself." This was another of my dad's proclamations that I heard repeatedly throughout my teenage years. He had his own priorities—beer and liquor, menthol cigarettes and pipe tobacco. On a sergeant's income he drove a gold Chrysler Imperial with white sidewall tires, rocket fins with bullet-shaped tail lights, and a fake continental kit with brushed aluminum on the trunk lid. Saving for some brat's college tuition was not in his plans.

Just because I graduated with awards, it didn't make me any wiser in practical matters. When a university application form asked whether I was a Nebraska resident or a non-resident, I was in a quandary because I equated "resident" with "native," which I was not. I was a minor, seventeen, and believed my legal resident status was the same as my parents, Wisconsin. As a non-resident I needlessly paid three times more tuition than I had to, which took every dollar I could scrape together from my savings, a scholarship, and a small loan I took out. My mom may have been right, all those times she called me an imbecile. I wasn't even smart enough to lie. It wasn't the dumbest thing I would ever do, by a long shot.

I didn't actually miss my parents with what you'd call being homesick. They didn't say they missed me either. I wasn't lonely until Cachito had to return to Peru. She was the only thing believable in this indifferent universe. The loss was devastating. I hadn't really thought through our inevitable separation. Some rule prohibited her return to America for two years, and we were both distraught. I got a passport with the idea of going to Peru. We exchanged letters on flimsy blue airmail stationary and plotted to meet in Panama at Christmas.

· · ·

I couldn't afford to keep my car running and over the summer I sold it, bringing in enough for one month's rent. I knew a guy named Mike whose roommate was drafted and soon on his way to Vietnam. Their place was improvised from half of a basement, a two-room box paneled in knotty-pine that was imaginatively termed an apartment. Splitting the rent with Mike cost me less than Mrs. Lohmeier's room did and it had a small kitchenette where I could heat up something from a can. It had a telephone and I could walk to work, so I moved in.

That's where I met Darlene Barnes in the early fall.

We were playing records and drinking beer with some friends that Darlene had come with. She looked cool. She had straight shoulder-length hair and one of her green eyes had a large golden spot on the iris. She wore a tight skirt and long wool stockings. She was sitting on the couch making out with my roommate.

"Hey, can I try that?" I asked.

"Sure," said Darlene, looking up with a friendly smile.

"Yeah, go ahead," Mike invited me, grinning and getting up to give me his place.

I sat down next to Darlene.

Dynamite.

Born in Texas, she had lived in France as a girl and sometimes wore a beret and smoked with the bored and indifferent air of someone in a French New Wave movie. Darlene was a year older, something of a mentor to me at times. As I spent more time with her I thought less about going to Peru to reunite with Cachito.

Together Darlene and I got to know some of Lincoln's outliers, an older avant-garde, including a few who would soon become national figures. We were riding around with her older cousins, and they stopped by to see a friend who was apparently living in his mother's basement. I recognized him as one of the motorcycling duo I had seen around town. He rode a 1950 Harley, it turned out. He was a Lincoln native six years older than me. By this time he already had a college degree in art and had been in the army prior to America's growing entanglement in Vietnam. We didn't have anything in common but I was interested in the stacks of his canvases leaning against the walls, paintings of pirates and Indians, cowboys and bikers. So far he was just plain Steve Wilson, soon to become famous as S. Clay Wilson.[1] (*See Endnotes*)

Classes began at the university, and after I prodded the old man, he kept his word about paying rent. His generosity was limited to twenty-five dollars a month, enough for me to live in cockroach-infested squalor. Poorer than I needed to be, I risked stealing a few of the more expensive textbooks, and often went without a meal.

At the beginning of the first semester I dropped off some poems for the student literary magazine, *Scrip*, sponsored by the English Department. In a few days the *Scrip* editor telephoned and invited me to meet. He didn't offer any comments about the poems. For that first encounter I walked to his apartment near campus, certain my work would be returned with a sad head shake.

I was expecting a haughty academic, but Steve Abbott was friendly and easy to talk to. He was a graduate student four years older than me, nearly as tall but not as thin as me. We sat on his front porch while we reviewed my poems and then he showed me some of the other submissions. There was a poem by someone named Murray Martz. Steve noted how the first verse ended with a long word, something like "incontrovertible" or "anthropomorphic," and indicated how the opening line of the following verse consisted of a simple and humble "I."

"See this," Steve pointed out, "how he juxtaposes the insignificance of his "I" with the previous broad landscape of a word." I nodded and wondered if Martz had explained it to Steve, or if Steve had spotted it on his own. I thought to myself that I didn't know the first thing about poetry and felt stupid about the writings I'd submitted. This would be the point when Steve handed them back and told me to try again for the next issue.

I was as bewildered as most people by the inscrutable lines of modern poetry. Only later did I see parallels with music and modern art, like when my friend Rich Johnston played a Deutsche Grammophon recording of *Gesang der Jünglinge* for me. It was outside any previous frame of reference. Karlheinz Stockhausen's electronic compositions were light years away from Motown and Nashville. Definitely not something that would germinate in the crushing emptiness of Nebraska's climate. I heard an eerie passage that made me think of flocks of birds dropping out of the sky, so I wrote a poem called "Oneday" using "icy bluebirds" as a metaphor for sleet and hail. The first verse went:

> *oneday drainspouts plummeted down*
> *icy bluebirds fell wingless to the blurry ground*
> *raving we splashed our footprints over the ravaged earth*
> *shielding our tormented faces from each mirrored sound*

Steve used three of my poems from that first meeting, including "Oneday." He printed some of my efforts in every issue of *Scrip* that year. He was a gentle soul, soft-spoken and somehow priestly, a native of Lincoln. I didn't have brothers but in the months that followed he became like a kindly older brother to me, or what I imagined an older brother to be like.

One time he brought out a gag snapshot of himself from his high-school days. It pictured him sitting in an old clawfoot bathtub in the snow in his family's back yard, wearing a vintage top hat and scrubbing his bare back with a long-handled bath brush. The comical stunt was like something I would do. As the year went on, Steve Abbott's[2] apartment evolved into the drop-in center of the university avant-garde, where I found many like-minded friends.

At Thanksgiving Darlene invited me to dinner with her family. Her dad was an Air Force officer who could afford to live in a big house in Lincoln instead of out at the crummy Air Force housing tract. Afterwards she brought me into the den and played me her Bob Dylan record albums. I'd heard "Subterranean Homesick Blues" and "Like a Rolling Stone" on the radio and so far that's all I knew about him. I was surprised to find out that he already had six albums.

Darlene often broadened my cultural education that way. When she said we ought to go live in a commune, I had to ask what a commune was. Through her I met the local president of Students for a Democratic Society. Carl Davidson[3] was a graduate student from Pennsylvania and lecturer at the university, an older guy with a luxurious droopy mustache and longish dark hair slicked back to his collar, who affected a black sport coat and a briar pipe. He was friendly enough, maybe at times a little condescending, as if I was one of his undergraduate students. He appeared at Steve Abbott's gatherings and I kept a tolerable truce with him. I only disliked that Darlene admired him so much.

He boosted membership in SDS by recruiting from our younger crowd. Darlene and our entire expanded circle of bohemian friends and acquaintances joined. All except me. I had a habit of independence and avoided so-called leaders and organized groups. Politics bored me, and I wasn't interested in studying propaganda literature. Language like "dialectics" and "Marxist" made my brain go numb. As far as I knew, Carl Davidson didn't write poetry or listen to electronic music, so there wasn't an artistic reason for me to be interested in him or SDS. It gave me a little bit of glee to irritate him by holding out. To be honest though, I couldn't afford the five-dollar membership fee. I wasn't respectable enough to be an official radical. But one weekend on Lincoln's main street, I did join a few dozen SDS members and others in a small protest march against apartheid in South Africa.

When Larry Clausen appeared at some of Steve Abbott's parties, I recognized him as the other half of the biker pair I'd seen, Steve Wilson's companion. He was a tall and brawny blonde who rode an Indian Chief motorcycle, a brand that wasn't made any more. He was also SDS chapter vice-president to Carl Davidson.

Unlike Wilson who never appeared, Clausen was congenial to us younger guys. He might have been too old to be drafted himself, or maybe like Wilson he'd already served. His advice to us was that if we were sent to Vietnam, to shoot our commanding officer. I couldn't tell if he was serious or joking, but I knew it wasn't something I could do. It happened though. They called it fragging. It expressed how we all felt about the entire military enterprise going on, not a bit as noble as World War II had been.

I had turned eighteen in September and by law had had to register for the draft the very same year that the military was building up Vietnam reinforcements in spectacular numbers. Although college students were still exempt from being drafted, I began to consider the possibility that I could be sent into combat. I hoped Vietnam would be over soon and I wouldn't have to worry about it.

The seeker side of me stayed watchful for a way to avoid the dead end of bourgeois convention. My opposition to the American status quo was instinctive, but affirmed by Darlene and the existence of Wilson, Abbott, Davidson, and Clausen—each in their own way an iconoclast.

CHAPTER 3

In the winter my roommate Mike was arrested for contributing to the delinquency of a minor, a fourteen-year-old girl. The court fined him and ordered him to move back in with his parents. Instead of getting a new roommate I found a bigger place with my guitar-playing friend Grady Waugh, who decided to move out of the student dorms. He was from western Nebraska where his dad was a prosperous rancher. We hit it off pretty good. He had a zany gleam in his eye and a good-natured laugh that kept my spirits up.

Our place on W Street was probably too big, too pricey, and too impractical for us: a parlor, a living room, a dining room, and a spacious kitchen. It came furnished with musty carpet and aged wallpaper, ancient yellow rollup window shades, shabby castoff sofas and side tables in the living and dining rooms. It had once been a two-story house and had an inside stairway to the basement. The original bedrooms were all in the upstairs apartment, so in our downstairs portion Grady and I staked out sleeping areas that weren't exactly a dorm room configuration. He took the exposed parlor by the front door and I took the cozy kitchen pantry, big enough to hold a cot and all my possessions.

Half of the rent was more than the twenty-five dollars I got from my dad and coughing up the extra amount promised to be a burden on my meager income. Almost immediately Pat Brougham asked if he could use the basement to work on his motorcycle. Its parts were soon scattered across the floor while he and his friend John Powers rebuilt it. We split the rent three ways—twenty-five dollars each— when Pat discovered a small nook that he cleaned out and moved into.

It was February 1966, and wind-driven snow swept across the prairie. When Steve Abbott heard that Allen Ginsberg was visiting Lawrence, Kansas, he drove down in his parents' car and invited the famous beatnik to come to Lincoln. I had read a City Lights copy of *Howl* and couldn't make much sense of it, but I was excited by the prospect of seeing Allen Ginsberg. I had no idea what he looked like. I expected a great writer to resemble Robert Frost or Carl Sandberg, or even Karl Shapiro, white-haired and dignified. Or because he was a beatnik he would wear a Basque beret and turtleneck sweater, and have a tidy Peter-Paul-and-Mary goatee.

Ginsberg initially appeared with two companions before a larger-than-usual crowd in the student union's lounge, in a section designated Hyde Park, where once a week students gathered around a microphone on a small dais. It was the university's concession to the recent Free Speech Movement on the Berkeley campus. When Ginsberg came, the entire area was standing-room-only, mobbed with students and faculty alike, curious to see the exotic visitor.

I was less than starstruck when I got my first look at the famous poet, not more than twenty feet from me. He was going on forty, only a year older than my dad, jelly-bellied and unimposing. His straggly dark hair was nearly shoulder-length but balding in front with a few remaining strands brushed across. He had a bushy beard and black-rimmed glasses. He was dumpy-looking in khakis and canvas shoes, a wrinkled white shirt with a couple of pens clipped into the pocket, and a rumpled tweed sport coat. So *that's* what a real beatnik looks like, I thought.

Ginsberg introduced his friends as Peter Orlovsky, who shared the minimal Hyde Park stage, and Peter's catatonic brother Julius, who sat quietly off to the side. Peter was several years younger than Ginsberg, more neatly dressed and better looking, quite handsome beneath his beatnik facade. He had a matter-of-fact, no-nonsense demeanor that I found likable. Peter wore glasses with thick black rims like Ginsberg's, and a Tibetan knit cap, blue jeans, and sandals. He was clean-shaven and had spectacular straight reddish hair down to his waist. Like an Indian holy man, he explained. I'd never seen a guy with hair as long as Peter's, and I thought it was pretty cool. We were all starting to skip haircuts and let our hair grow wild by then, encouraged by the Beatles on the cover of their new *Rubber Soul* album. Even the girls were giving up their short bouffants for a Joan Baez, Marianne Faithfull style of long straight hair.

At first Ginsberg talked about how he'd been voted the King of May in Czechoslovakia the year before. Peter, a former army medic, told us that he had rescued Julius from a mental hospital and now cared for him.

Then Ginsberg began to talk about writing. "Peter and I were experimenting with a new method."

"To get more authentic dialog," Peter added.

"When we were in bed together we'd stop and write down our conversation. We wanted to get the intimate language," Ginsberg explained.

"I wrote what he said and he wrote what I said."

"At first it worked pretty well," said Allen, "but then we got too passionate and carried away. We couldn't stop to write anything down."

When the crowd laughed, I laughed along. It was a performance they'd worked out for public occasions so as not to outrage anyone, yet at the same time unsettling the quaint Nebraskans—myself included. I thought, *What the heck is this?* It wasn't a topic you heard much about yet. Technically, their conduct was against the law, but not enforced, and there was no law against talking about it. It surprised me that they didn't seem effeminate or talk with a lisp. I decided to try to be more open-minded. Later I wondered why they needed to mention it at all, since it had nothing to do with poetry. I reasoned that they could have used a tape recorder, and decided it was their way of announcing their forbidden relationship.

Ginsberg then spoke at length about Zen. At one point he excused himself for a moment to pull out a handkerchief and said, "Blowing the nose is also highest perfect wisdom." To warm up for reading he played finger cymbals and chanted. For his contribution, Peter sat cross-legged on the floor beside him and played a portable Indian harmonium. As a preview of the reading he would give to a larger audience in the auditorium, Ginsberg read from a work he was composing called "Wichita Vortex Sutra." He read excerpts from another long poem in progress he called "Auto Poesy to Nebraska" and concluded the afternoon with some question-and-answer.

That evening Ginsberg, Peter, and Julius were dinner guests at a fraternity house. Steve Abbott invited me to join the entourage, knowing how badly I needed a meal. As he and I crossed the street with the Ginsberg trio I felt privileged to be part of the bohemian group. At the dinner there were a couple of other professors and non-fraternity students as guests, but I was the only undergraduate, and distinctly out of place. Unlike myself, who never had a sit-down meal any more, the stereotypical frat guys were well-fed, clean-cut and nicely dressed. They often had new cars, and got wads of money from home. I simultaneously disdained them and envied them. They weren't the kind whose fathers told them, "When you turn eighteen, you're on your own."

In the swanky dining hall, with its beamed ceilings and lustrous wainscoting, Ginsberg sat at another table and Peter and Julius were at mine. Someone asked Peter if he also wrote poetry.

"I do," he said. "I have some in a book called *The New American Poetry 1945-1960*."

"I think I have that book," I said to him from across the table. What were the odds? I supposed that was something a New York Beat

Poet didn't expect to hear from some kid out in the middle of the Great Waste Land of Nebraska.

"The one with the American flag on the cover," said Peter.

"Yeah, that's the one," I said. It was a thick anthology from University of California Press, edited by Donald Allen. I wasn't sure I had actually read Orlovsky's poem, so when I got home I opened the book and read it again. It didn't exactly split the sky asunder. Something about sweeping the floor and washing dishes. My own poems weren't much worse.

A large private gathering was planned for Ginsberg and his friends and we wanted the prestige of having it at our place on W Street. At my invitation Steve Abbott brought over two carloads of professors and graduate students, Carl Davidson among them. Into our domain marched the self-appointed reconnaissance committee of hip intellectuals modulated by bourgeois respectability, scouting out the venue. Although Steve lived closer to campus with his roommate Dan Ortiz and had frequent parties at their place, their two bedrooms were kept shut, whereas Grady and I had four large wide-open rooms. The survey crew judged our location better suited for the expected crowd size and after looking around they gave their nod of approval.

After his formal reading in the auditorium the next day, Ginsberg arrived at our door with Julius and Peter Orlovsky, escorted by Steve Abbott and Karl Shapiro. Our party to celebrate his visit was underway and I welcomed him in from the cold. I gripped his hand and he said to me "My hand doesn't exist. You're shaking a cloud." I chuckled, although in the flutter of greetings I didn't question him further about his scrap of wisdom. In fact I would have liked to talk more about Ginsberg's cryptic remark, knowing well enough that he wasn't trying to be funny. It was the sort of mystical consciousness I wanted to write poems about, and I was just beginning to puzzle it out for myself.

To me Ginsberg represented a world of lofty aspirations beyond the shiny cars, tidy lawns, and *Good Housekeeping* living rooms of my mid-America surroundings. Those material comforts were a madness destroying us all, fitting correlates of the white-bread character of Nebraska, of absurd religious beliefs and God-is-on-our-side patriotism. All of that Establishment conformity was a surrender of the will. It was a mass hypnosis to which I wasn't about to compromise my independence.

Ginsberg and Karl Shapiro took shelter in the side parlor that served as Grady's room, facing each other in a *tête-à-tête* from the edges of the twin beds. To my disappointment they remained there under the dazzling ceiling light surrounded by standing-room-only onlookers. I had hoped they would be circulating and I'd have a chance to approach them in the shifting clusters that parties formed, but I yielded a place in the parlor to other guests. The bulk of the crowd surged and swirled past the parlor and through our two living rooms to a beer keg in the kitchen. I'd already heard Ginsberg read twice and had met Karl Shapiro before, and I was too distracted by my friends and the beer keg to linger and listen attentively.

Peter Orlovsky wasn't in the parlor either. Like any domestic partner, he'd heard Ginsberg's routine often enough to know everything he was going to say. Instead he circulated around the party, checking frequently on his immobile catatonic brother. Julius wore a rumpled black suit and sat in a straight-backed wooden chair the entire time. He held a beer and smiled vaguely at us, and said nothing. A trickle of spittle occasionally ran from the corner of his mouth, but they said he was better off with Peter than being locked away. Peter mothered and brothered him and took him everywhere. For me too this was a better scene, much improved over being locked away with my parents, or in any fraternity house. Only difference was, I didn't have someone to look after me the way Julius did.

Our usual cadre of undergraduate bohemians had gathered. A lot of English Department academics were in attendance, the types in corduroys and tweed sport coats with leather elbow patches. A few people who had trailed Ginsberg up from Kansas were there as well. I had no idea who any of them were.

I saw an unfamiliar black guy about my age standing nearby, wearing a blue work shirt and a sheepskin vest. In those days though, nobody said "black guy." We said "spade." In 1966 people in Nebraska said "colored person," so I think he would have agreed he was a spade. It wasn't meant to be derogatory, and neither was calling girls chicks. Spade, cat, chick, pad, bread, square, and cool were part of the hip lingo. Dig it, daddy-o. He looked friendly and I asked him if I could bum a smoke.

"Yeah, sure," he said, breaking into a toothy grin and shaking a Marlboro out of a red and white flip-top box. He was tall like me, though more athletic looking, and wore glasses with thick black frames like everyone wore: Allen Ginsberg and Peter Orlovsky, Steve Abbott and Karl Shapiro, Grady and me.

"Thanks, man."

The black guy handed me his cigarette to light mine from and said, "Cool party. You from Lincoln?"

"Yeah, this here is my place. I go to the university. What about you?"

"I saw Ginsberg in Lawrence, Kansas last week and came up so I could see him again."

"No kidding. Wow. Yeah, I heard some Kansas people came up here. I'm Randy, by the way."

"Joe Knight," he said as we shook hands.

I introduced him to Darlene, Grady, and a few others. A day or two later Joe Knight went back to Kansas long enough to fetch a few personal things, then returned to stay in Lincoln and become part of our crowd, sleeping on Steve Abbott's couch.

As our party began winding down Peter Orlovsky lent a hand with the cleanup. He was quite domestic in helping straighten our place, collecting paper cups and emptying ashtrays while chatting with Darlene and me. Although he looked exotic with his long red hair, he was thoughtful and considerate, a very responsible person, not at all like you imagined a beatnik.

I saw Allen Ginsberg and Karl Shapiro to the door with a polite goodbye, and thanked them for coming. I shook hands again with Ginsberg and noticed his finger stroking my palm. I'd read in a book somewhere that this was a gay signal so I pretended not to notice. His lecherous gesture wasn't the spiritual action of a holy cloud and it managed to frighten me off.

An older and more worldly me would have good-naturedly said, "Behave yourself, Allen," and prolonged our goodbye. In fact I could have made myself memorable to both poets, said welcome to my humble abode, here's some of my own poetry by the way, send me a post card, keep in touch, come back again, yakety-yak. At eighteen, I was sheepish before these formidable men. Maybe I heard an echo of my mom, the inner critic I lived with. She would have reminded me that an imbecile—her typical word for me—had no business imposing on these Distinguished Men of Letters, even in my own home. And yet three years later Doubleday would publish *The Writing on the Wall*, an anthology of protest poetry. It included a work of mine appearing alongside Ginsberg and a legion of venerated American writers.

Not long after the big party for Allen Ginsberg, the landlord took us unaware when he dropped over to inspect the furnace one morning. Instead of using the indoor stairs from our kitchen, he entered the basement by the outside steps and discovered Pat sleeping there. The basement wasn't part of the rental contract and he told us Pat had to clear out. Grady and I couldn't afford the rent by ourselves, so in March all three of us slipped away in separate directions without giving notice.

CHAPTER 4

I walked to a weathered house with peeling paint on North 17th, where the same For Rent sign was perpetually tacked next to a screen door on the covered front porch. Our house on W Street had been partitioned into an upper and lower apartment. This one was even more fragmented into five assorted living spaces. The manager led me up a steep unlit stairway squeezed between high walls to look at a furnished attic room. Even if the location was two blocks from the university campus, it was clear why the For Rent sign had hung outside for so long. The squalid garret had sloping ceilings, old water-stained floral wallpaper, a buckled and scuffed linoleum floor. There was a steam radiator for heat, and a window with a gray winter view of rooftops and a gravel alley. There was a small sink and a two-burner gas stove. The shared bathroom was downstairs on the second floor. It was the perfect setting for a destitute young poet.

"How much is the rent?"

"Thirty-five dollars."

"Oh." I guessed I couldn't afford it. I said, "I'm only used to paying twenty-five." I wasn't bargaining, only stating a fact.

He thought a moment, probably calculating how long it would be before any other prospective renter appeared, and said, "Well, this place is only worth twenty-five anyway."

. . .

Darlene brought a large painting by the motorcycle artist Steve Wilson and we hung it over the bed. It was signed "S. Clay Wilson." I didn't ask her how she got him to part with his painting, but I guessed she didn't tell him it was for me. In the foreground four outlaw bikers stood as a group with the upper parts of their motorcycles visible— the handlebars, seats, and gas tanks. In the background was a roadside diner with a sign for Tree Frog Beer. The bikers in the painting had the renegade look of the time, more up-to-date than Marlon Brando in *The Wild One*, but not quite the uniformed appearance of Hells Angels either. A couple wore sunglasses. One had a cigarette hanging on his lip. Another had a button on his jacket with the number 13 on it.

"What's that?" I asked her. "Why's it say 13?"

"The thirteenth letter of the alphabet. M. It stands for marijuana." Like I said, Darlene filled gaps in my knowledge with regularity, although in this case none of us had actually had any marijuana yet. Maybe Wilson did. Maybe there was some to be found even in Lincoln.

It was nearly a year since I'd left my parents. I was lucky to have the part-time delivery job that I'd had in high school. It was keeping me afloat as a college freshman. The boss ribbed me about my uncut hair, but kept me on because he already knew I was dependable. But then my fellow drivers got into four separate crashes in a matter of weeks. No injuries, just enough to do damage. Because of the wrecks the owner had to let everyone go who was under twenty-one in order to keep his insurance on the four International Scouts. So now I didn't have an income for even the smallest amount of groceries. At 6' 2", I didn't know my weight but guessed it around 130 or less.

I didn't mind working but you couldn't get hired anywhere unless you had a haircut. I went hungry rather than give up my principles. We let our hair grow untamed, savages who defied the bourgeoisie. I felt akin to native Americans, Vikings, and Merovingians. Even the presidents on our money had long hair, and patriotic legends like General Custer and Buffalo Bill Cody. The Establishment identified us as effeminate hippies and draft dodgers. The cops routinely stopped us to check our ID, people in cars honked their horns and threw things. Others taunted us with "Are you a boy or a girl?" and other witty repartee. I was a Samson among Philistines.

I mailed a letter to my parents about being let go from work, not really expecting much help from them, and they sent an extra five dollars. I still had my military dependent ID card and a friend drove me out to the Air Force base where I could buy groceries cheap at the commissary. I wrote back to my parents.

> For $4.83 I bought 20 pounds of potatoes, 1 box of rice, 1 box of oatmeal, 13 cans of soup, 2 cans of beans, 3 cans of spaghetti, 5 oranges, 4 apples, 1 loaf of bread, 1 jar of peanut butter. I'm going to feast. This is more than I've had in the past two months. The way I've survived is every day somebody takes pity on me and gives me something like maybe a sandwich. I really owe my existence to this girlfriend who keeps smuggling some food out of her folks' cupboard and bringing it over.

Eventually Darlene's parents found out she was stealing food for me and they told her to just take me the food, that she didn't have to sneak it out of the house.

In the aftermath of Allen Ginsberg's controversial visit, I was about to join the Mimeo Revolution. Nobody called it that at the time, or if they did I hadn't heard of it and I wasn't part of it. With no precedent or peer group of collaborators, the idea came to me after helping Steve Abbot run off the next *Scrip* on a mimeograph. I decided to risk buying enough materials to print a collection of my own poems to sell for profit. I needed the money for more groceries.

I typed fifty poems on mimeograph stencils, enough for twenty-five two-sided pages. After some coaxing, my friend Grady wrote an introduction. He began with, "The Rhody Poetry Revolution is at hand," and recounted a dream I once told him about, in which I was inching my way up a narrow stairway that strongly resembled the one to my apartment. I was being followed by a stealthy crowd. Each time I stopped and turned to look they stopped too, formed little cocktail-party conversation groups below me, and pretended that they weren't following. I was surprised and pleased with Grady's words. I didn't ask him why he signed his introduction "Jerome" instead of Grady Waugh. Maybe he thought it was creative. In my paranoid moments I thought it was so his name wouldn't be associated with my drivel.

The dream that Grady wrote about sort of reminded me of an incident when I was in sixth grade. We were supposed to write a short story, a page or two long, and then read it to our classmates the next day. Two girls collaborated on a single long story, and took turns reading it to us. Their story was about our class, and each one of us had a small role. Hearing everyone's names and what they did in the story had us listening intently, especially for our own names.

Our class was trapped in a haunted-house dungeon. In the dark underground some kids joked, others sat dumb and helpless, others were in tears. My part in the story came as I inched along the walls and studied them with care. I discovered a hidden control that opened a door and everyone escaped up a stairway.

I was pleased that the girls acknowledged my reputation as one of the kids in class who kept his head and figured things out. More than that, I liked that when our situation began to look hopeless I was able to help everyone. I wanted to do that in real life somehow. It felt like a pronouncement upon me. It was a story that I couldn't forget. I hadn't heard of Plato's allegory of the cave yet, but the resemblance was there.

. . .

Steve Abbott was an accomplished cartoonist, and illustrated *Scrip* with his hand-drawn ads for the downtown businesses that contributed sponsor money. He drew some practice sketches of me, and then a final version on a stencil for a cover page illustration, including the title, *A Year's Worth of Wonder: 1965-1966.* I mimeoed the cover on gray construction paper and side-stapled the book's pages together.

My intent was to sell about eighty copies for fifty cents each to recover cost of materials and make a small profit. At a price of one cent per poem, it was a bargain. I saved the other twenty copies to give away. The book included "Ashes," one of the poems I'd had in the October *Scrip:*

> *when my gleaming*
> *selfly being*
> *ceased to be*
> > *i found my shadow*
> > *flicked*
> > *across the sea*
> > *unseen thus*
> > *challenged by*
> > *nothing*
> > > *but my*
> > > *termination*
> > > *of determination*
> > *on the edge*
> > *of cold*
> > > *dancing among*
> > > *the sensations*

There might have been some logic to the way I divided and indented the lines of "Ashes." A critical analysis would point out how the second two verses were "flicked" inward, and the last two lines "danced" away from the margin. Or else I subconsciously reverted to eighth-grade exercises of diagramming sentences. That in itself would be an admissible technique. If Jackson Pollock could make a career out of dripping paint, why not gain notoriety writing poetry as diagrammed sentences?

At the time of my printed collection I also memorialized Allen Ginsberg's visit in a poem and gave it to Steve along with four other poems for possible use in *Scrip.* He used them all in the March-April issue, including my untitled Ginsberg poem, five verses. He had originally planned to include Ginsberg's "Auto Poesy to Nebraska" in the issue.

"This is the best SCRIP to date and will probably become a collector's item, if it already isn't," began Karl Shapiro in his review of *Scrip* in the April 7 campus newspaper, the *Daily Nebraskan.* The headline was "The Best Ever." Further down he wrote:

> Randy Rhody writes one of the best tribute poems. Terry Tilford and Jeff Atcheson help beef up the issue.... Mr. Rhody has also published his first book of poems which is being sold with the SCRIP for fifty cents. Steve Abbott deserves a double bandolier of holy medals for the work he has done...

I was flattered that Shapiro was aware of my book and slipped a mention of it into his article. I wondered if he associated my name with the kid who had once interviewed him, or with the party on W Street. Shapiro also called out some campus rancor about Ginsberg's visit:

> The Visitor donated his fine poem "Auto Poesy to Nebraska" to SCRIP but it could not be included in the contents proper. Some establishmentarian technicality intervened. But the poem is included as a supplement.
>
> N.B. One of the bookstores has removed the Ginsberg supplement and filed it in the trash can. No matter.

Terry Tilford, also mentioned in Shapiro's article, followed up on the controversial Ginsberg supplement a few days later with a letter in the Campus Opinion column of the *Daily Nebraskan*:

> The new issue of *Scrip* magazine is now on sale, and congratulations are in order for several interested parties: to Steve Abbott and his staff...to Randy Rhody... and lastly, to Our Chairman, who, with a stolid determination approaching missionary fervor, forbid the appearance in this issue of Allen Ginsberg's "Auto Poesy to Nebraska," on the remarkable and shifting ground that it is not student work... forcing Mr. Abbott and his associates to issue the poem as a free supplement to the magazine itself.

"Auto Poesy to Nebraska" did indeed come out as a supplement. Within a few months, it would also surface in a small mimeograph publication from Omaha that included poetry of mine.

I suspected censorship also sabotaged my attempt to sell my poetry. Each time a new *Scrip* came out—four or five that academic year—a temporary sales table was set up in the student union for a week, tended in shifts by some of the writers who were represented in the magazine. As Karl Shapiro had noted, *A Year's Worth of Wonder* was for sale there too. About thirty-five copies sold, before the cardboard box with the remaining copies went missing. No one at the sales table knew where it was. First I looked nearby, thinking someone had absent-mindedly set it elsewhere in the room. Then I asked around the English Department offices, checking with a few of the professors. If some administrator mistakenly confiscated them in the process of policing the Ginsberg "Auto Poesy to Nebraska" insert, I was never advised. I didn't use profanity in my own writing, so I assumed the worst—that someone took them because it was bad poetry, and threw them in the trash. Of the original hundred copies, almost half of them vanished. The mimeo revolution was suppressed, locally anyway. Whatever profit I made on the few sales didn't keep me in groceries for very long.

. . .

"Come out to Kearney State and do a poetry reading with me." Terry Tilford, of the defiant Campus Opinion letter, was one of the other poets on the *Scrip* staff with Steve Abbott. He was a junior, had fiery hair and a bristling red beard. I'd seen him lately at some of Steve's parties and gotten to know him better.

"What kind of reading?" I said. "I mean, read to who?"

"My friend teaches English Lit there. He invited me to read to his class, except I don't want to go alone."

"Ha. Read to a college class? Not me, man." My writing was an introverted pursuit. Reading was a performing art, too public and exposed for comfort.

"Come on, it'll be just for an hour. And talk a little bit about our work."

"I don't know about that." I was flattered to be asked though. After all, I had won a high-school prize for best poetry. Been published in four different issues of *Scrip*. Met Allen Ginsberg and Karl Shapiro. Published and sold my own work. Reading at Kearney would be added experience. If I wanted to be a poet, I knew I had to do it, and I let myself be persuaded in spite of doubts.

Terry drove us to Kearney State University, about 130 miles west of Lincoln. In an ordinary classroom twenty or thirty students not much older than me sat in the kind of wooden chairs with a built-in writing surface on one arm. We weren't as impressive as Allen Ginsberg, but we presented ourselves as real poets rather than mere ordinary students who wrote poetry. I hid my nervousness and read my poems with neither fear of ridicule nor arrogant authority.

After our readings we answered questions about how long it took to write a poem, or what things inspired us to write, or how we determined that a poem was finished. A letter-sweater jock asked me, "When you write a poem do you feel like you've accomplished something?"

That caught me off guard. I said, "Yes," without elaborating. *Next question.* A better reply would've been that I thought of writing as a continuous practice rather than in terms of accomplishment. If I wrote enough bad poems I'd occasionally produce a few that were good.

On the drive back to Lincoln I wondered if he had been taunting me with his question. I asked Terry what he thought. "You didn't go there to debate your work. You aren't play-acting at being a poet. You're the real thing." I supposed the varsity guy hadn't left home at seventeen and he wasn't getting through college with his own money like me.

When I told Steve Abbott about our trip and the guy's question, he said I should have answered, "When you catch a football do you feel like you've accomplished something?"

I was surrounded by writers, artists, musicians, and filmmakers. "I seem to be the center of aesthetics around here," I wrote, and then complained:

> ...every time somebody writes something, they want me to read it, they expect authoritative criticisms, and I don't know anything either. One friend of mine, the editor of SCRIP... did half a dozen drawings and sketches of me, and then had me sit for an oil-on-canvas painting... Another guy... filmed me shaving, and filmed me eating a hamburger. He's planning on doing an hour long film of me reading a book. Real crazy.

Rich Johnston was the filmmaker, the same guy who had turned me on to Karlheinz Stockhausen's electronic music. Out with his camera one night near downtown, we appropriated a grocery cart left along the sidewalk to use as a prop. I climbed into it and Rich filmed Joe Knight pushing me along, an absurdist stunt similar to sitting in a bathtub in the snow, a surreal sort of Luis Buñuel performance. A light rain had turned to fine mist and streetlight reflections on the wet pavement would make the black-and-white film more interesting than it was. A cop stopped to see what we were doing and took all three of us in, minus the shopping cart. At the police station we stood around a detective's desk while he took the officer's report. Rich continued filming, so I improvised for his camera and slouched against the wall like a sullen perp, making our situation into theater. They decided there was nothing to charge us with and sent us away.

A few weeks later Rich set up a projector and screen in the student union building and held a public viewing of his silent films, including the shopping cart-police station one, for about thirty or forty interested people. A girl I didn't know very well who worked on the *Scrip* editing staff came over to me afterwards. She said I might be interested that a guy in Omaha, Matt Shulman, was putting together a poetry magazine, and wrote down his address for me.

I stopped by the first floor to pay my rent and the apartment manager invited me in to have a beer, even though he knew I was under age. Bob and his wife Paula were from southern California, and his pencil-thin Errol Flynn mustache set him apart from Lincoln natives. Other than that they looked pretty ordinary. They were so much older compared to me that I was kind of flattered that they spent time talking to me. I had told them about my poetry and the party for Allen Ginsberg. Bob had been impressed when I showed him the Wilson motorcycle painting in my room. He worked on the staff at the university art museum and was a painter himself. He told me about his plein air days in southern California.

"Yeah man, I used to stroll across the road along the ocean, with all those people in cars on their way to work, and I'd go up in the hills and get high and paint."

As the three of us sat in their living room Bob and Paula decided to turn me on. They must have considered me a safer risk than the native Cornhuskers that surrounded us.

"You ever smoked pot?" he asked.

"No. What's it like?" I knew about pot but I didn't know anyone who had any, let alone anyone who smoked it. Just a few weeks before, Timothy "turn on, tune in, drop out" Leary had been sentenced to thirty years in prison for possession of less than half an ounce.

"It makes you real mellow, man. You wanna try some?"

"Yeah sure, I'll try it." I was grateful to have the experience.

"We'll roll a joint and get high." He got out a cigar box with some rolling papers and a sandwich bag containing some shredded leaves and rolled a joint, the way my grandpa used to roll his cigarettes with Bugler tobacco. Lighting it up, they took turns demonstrating how to smoke it.

"Hold it in your lungs like this and try not to cough. Then pass it back."

I didn't know what to expect. After we passed it around a few times I began to feel a little drifty. It was weird, not the same as getting drunk. We smoked it only that one time, or maybe a couple more times. I kept their secret to myself, knowing they could go to prison for having it. Call it M, call it 13. It made me feel somehow like a cloud that didn't exist.

It continued to bug me that Darlene was infatuated with Carl Davidson. During second semester she rented a room in the same four-story fleabag hotel downtown where he lived on the floor above her. Probably most of the building was student-occupied. Immersing themselves in the proletariat, I figured. Bathroom down the hall. At night you could listen to the radiator banging. Sometimes in the morning she'd go upstairs to make breakfast in Carl's kitchenette and bring it down to me. But it didn't take much imagination to suspect she was upstairs exploring New Left politics and other matters on nights when I wasn't there.

Darlene might have been my quasi-girlfriend for a few months, partly drawn to my poet persona, though she wasn't my exclusive girl for long. Her way of acquiring and discarding quarry made the love-em-and-leave-em guys look amateur. The Women's Lib movement was still a few years in the future. Darlene was a pioneer, seeking out campus intellectuals and arty bohemian types of which I was only one specimen.

I decided to skip classes and hitchhike to Omaha to find the guy with the poetry magazine. I told myself I wanted to get published somewhere besides in *Scrip*. The real reason was that Darlene reclaimed her Steve Wilson motorcycle gang painting and ceased her overnight stays in my attic room. She brought a little twerp no one had seen before over to Steve Abbott's where we were all hanging out. Some people ignored him out of sympathetic allegiance to me, but I was wounded that a few traitors acted friendly to him. As a girlfriend she was a source of grief and misery. She was a character, had turned me on to a lot of things, but also turned me inside out. It gave me more incentive to get away from Lincoln.

Even if hitchhiking couldn't be very difficult, I needed moral support, and Joe Knight had experience hitchhiking between Kansas and Lincoln—so he said. He was having girlfriend troubles of his own and after some coaxing agreed to come with me. I packed a duffel bag with a change of clothes, a comb and a toothbrush, a loaf of bread, a spiral notepad to write in, a paperback book to read, and some copies of my poetry book, *A Year's Worth of Wonder 1965-1966*. I told Bob and Paula I'd be away, in case they noticed I wasn't around.

PART II

CHICAGO AND CLEVELAND

CHAPTER 5

Joe and I got out on the highway between Lincoln and Omaha beneath an overcast morning sky and watched the steady traffic flowing past. We might have looked like a modern-day Jim and Huck Finn. Motorists more likely viewed us as possible serial killers. Peoples' memories were still fresh with a riveting episode of recent Nebraska history. A few years before my family moved to Nebraska, nineteen-year-old Charles Starkweather had killed eleven people on a murder spree in Lincoln. He'd gone to my high school, but the yearbooks and trophy cases didn't mention him. In 1959, five months after he went to the electric chair in Lincoln, the *In Cold Blood* murders that Truman Capote wrote about transpired just next door in Kansas. Whether we were picturesque or not, drivers saw little need to stop for two risky-looking fellows like Joe and me.

An old-timer in a worn pickup truck finally pulled over and said he was taking a side road but it would get us some distance closer. We were desperate and hopped in. We regretted it later after he dropped us off. The two-lane route had less traffic on it and the prospect of another ride diminished. When we got a short lift back to the main highway, we were about fifteen miles and two hours from where we'd left it. We did more walking along the four-lane road bordered with power lines and barb-wire fences. In the afternoon we went up a gravel drive to a farmhouse to ask for some water but no one came to the door. Instead we each helped ourselves to an apple from some bushel baskets on the porch.

It was fifty miles to Omaha but it took us most of the day.

We got into town and arrived at Matt Shulman's house in a rundown neighborhood, unannounced and unintroduced. I was prepared to encounter a polished and urbane entrepreneur of the publishing industry. A scruffy guy in his mid-twenties with a slight beard answered the door, looking as unprofitable as everyone else I knew.

"I'm looking for Matt Shulman," I said.

"That's me," he answered.

"I heard you publish poetry." I told him about the girl at the film screening who'd given me his name. "We just hitchhiked from Lincoln to look for you."

I knew that in his mind we didn't look like the undesirables that all those passing drivers on the highway took us for. He'd probably never heard of Charles Starkweather. He could tell by our looks that we were cool, and welcomed us into a place that looked like the usual sparse habitats I was used to.

"Yeah, I'm getting together some poetry for printing in a journal soon," he said. "It's going to be called *Do-It!*."

"I've been writing poems for our magazine at the university." I got a copy of my mimeographed book out and handed it to him. "A couple months ago I printed my poems. I was hoping you could use something."

"Wow, this is great. I'm sure I can use some, yes. Or you can give me some newer ones." It didn't seem like he was going to be judgmental or debate whether to print one. He didn't ask if I thought I accomplished anything when I wrote a poem. I was excited about the chance to get in print somewhere outside of Lincoln.

"You ever hear of the *Marrahwanna Quarterly*?" he asked me.

"Nope."

"It's from Cleveland. Wait, I'll show you." He went in another room and came back with a side-stapled pamphlet of twenty or so mimeographed pages that looked nothing like *Scrip* did.

Smudges showed where errors on the stencils had been typed over, and the page layouts were careless. Some were crammed with text and had narrow margins. There were amateurish drawings. The poems were defiant political rants, contained obscenities, spoke of drugs and cops. From the lines that I glanced through, I gathered that a lot of authors weren't any better than me. My own writing would fit right in.

"It's put out by d. a. levy." He wrote his name in lowercase letters like e. e. cummings did. Darryl Levy was his name. "He prints a lot of other people's work. You ought to go see him."

"I might." He wrote down Levy's address for me and I considered since I'd come this far, I just might keep going.

Matt explained he was from Cleveland and was living in Omaha doing some Great Society, War on Poverty, government program work with Job Corps or VISTA.

Later he rolled a joint that the three of us shared, standing in his kitchen, giggling and saying "Oh wow!" It was the second or third time I smoked pot and the sensation was still unfamiliar. I had a weird impression that I took a giant step across the linoleum and said some nonsense words. I didn't know if I really had or if I only imagined I had.

Joe and I slept on the floor and in the morning Matt guided us around the neighborhood to look for a poet he knew, Clarence Major. He told us that Clarence had published a literary magazine in Chicago for a while, *Coercion Review*, that featured poets and writers such as Henry Miller, Kenneth Patchen and Lawrence Ferlinghetti. First we went to Clarence's sister's house where he was staying. He wasn't there and we walked a few blocks to a shabby storefront where a few winos seemed to be living. I was impressed to see every level surface and window sill covered with empty wine bottles glowing green in the morning sun. No one there knew where he was. We checked other places and located him at last.

Clarence Major was about 30, a black man with a goatee and mustache, amiable to us younger guys, not high-handed. If anything he seemed unassuming. I liked that we were dissimilar and yet shared a common interest in writing. If I had stayed at Matt's for more than a day, perhaps I'd have seen more of him. I was humbled by Clarence's greater experience and deferential to the gap in our ages, and didn't presume to find out more about him or suggest keeping in contact.[1] In an orbit where I sought belonging, Clarence might have been an encouraging influence, as Karl Shapiro and Allen Ginsberg would have, had I broached it to any of them, the times we met.

I persuaded Joe to continue east with me to Cleveland to find d. a. levy instead of going back to Lincoln. We decided to take a bus as far as we had money for—less than two hundred miles to Grinnell, Iowa, which we'd heard was a cool place. At the Grinnell College campus we walked around and made friends with some guys we hung out with for the afternoon. For dinner they smuggled us something to eat from the student cafeteria and let us sleep overnight on their dorm room floor. Someone must have ratted on us, because the next day a school administrative type in a suit waylaid Joe and me to politely let us know that the school had overnight guest rooms. He wasn't a jerk about it, just doing his job and probably had better things to do than enforce petty rules. I wondered if he meant the rooms were free but didn't ask. We thanked him for the information, as if we could afford rooms, and said we were leaving anyway.

We cut through a parking lot and walked past a well-dressed couple who'd brought their son for a tour of the campus. They asked if we were students and I said I was, in Lincoln, not at Grinnell. The three of them were driving back to Chicago, about a four-and-a-half-hour trip, so I asked if we could get a ride. In the car I wondered what kind of parents would take their son college hunting.

. . .

Before Lincoln we lived among civilians in a college town where my dad spent some time as an Air Force recruiter. I was in eighth grade, my second year in the junior high school, a four-story brick fortress. A few times I was summoned from class to spend an hour in a private office with a man who gave me a mix of aptitude and psychology tests. He seemed more friendly than most grownups and I enjoyed the sessions. I took a vocabulary test that continued until I missed three words in a row, and he said I had gotten to "the superior adult level." He wanted to place me in an advanced English class.

Talk about vocabulary. At home I heard words that were banned from TV in the inexplicable tirades my mom unwound on me. If no one else was around, her vocabulary could be salted with more obscenities than Allen Ginsberg's most notorious poem. It was language I wasn't supposed to know yet, out of proportion to any infractions I may have committed. *Sticks and stones*, I told myself at the time.

At one meeting the school counselor predicted that I could go to MIT some day. I asked him what MIT was, and his answer worried me, though I said nothing. The idea of technology, whatever that was, didn't sound interesting. And an institute sounded institutional, as when my mom would say to me, "You belong in an institution." I let him persuade me to jump from math and join the algebra class for advanced kids, but I declined to take advanced English because I thought I'd be overwhelmed with homework from both classes.

A few days after the testing sessions the principal called me in for a one-on-one meeting. It was a big school and I knew he didn't do that for everybody. I wasn't used to people showing an interest in me. It made me a little uneasy, like being King of Valentines, like something was expected of me that I knew I couldn't produce. He asked me what I wanted to do when I grew up. The correct response must have been something that required an MIT degree. I said I'd like to be a stock car racer.

The men at school must have wondered why I got Bs and Cs

instead of straight As. They called my parents in for a private meeting. Afterwards I asked what the visit was about and my mom answered that the people at school said I should be getting better grades. I guess some other truths likely hadn't come out at that meeting with the school officials. "You imbecile!" my mom would rage at me, along with the dirty words. Never, "My Valentine!" For his part, my dad would shake me while my head bobbled and my teeth rattled. The contradictions between school and home, not to mention the frequent moves, left me with a cynical view of life.

Instead of mentioning MIT or other encouragement, my parents frightened me with threats to send me away to a military boarding school. Later they dropped that idea, and my mom shifted to telling me I belonged in reform school, a prison for boys. Some place with damp cells, bad food, and regular beatings. An institution.

In the summer she took my sister away to stay with my grandparents, abandoning me with less sentiment than leaving a potted plant. When school started they didn't return and my dad and I stayed on in the house.

Ninth grade began just before my fourteenth birthday. I was nervous about the first day of school. My dad was already dressed in his Air Force uniform and having coffee and a cigarette when I came downstairs and made my usual cereal and toast. Afterwards I went back upstairs to get something in my room and for some reason stepped into my parents' bedroom. A strange woman with reddish hair was sleeping there, or pretending to sleep, her bare shoulders uncovered by the white sheets.

Returning downstairs, I asked my dad who she was. He didn't explain but announced that he and my mom were considering divorce. I guess I was expected to fill in a lot of blanks myself about the redhead. My dad smoked his cigarette while I sniffled. I was disgusted that a few tears escaped me in spite of myself. Not because a happy home was about to be destroyed. No, happy memories were non-existent. My grief was because I hated them both for the lousy ways they had mistreated me and this confirmed what a disaster my parents were. The news gouged the old wound of their betrayal in Alaska nine years before.

What a great back-to-school birthday present. I composed myself and walked the mile to school alone. I could handle it. People got divorced all the time. Still, I didn't tell anyone about it, not my friends or anyone at school. Even if these shameful secrets were someone else's, not mine, I felt obligated to keep them concealed. It would have been a good story for the school counselor and the principal.

My dad was more stealthy after that, since I never saw the woman again. We soon moved into a moldy, cockroach-ridden second story apartment in an old house nearer school and the downtown. I enjoyed not having my mom nagging at me, and my dad was easier to live with. I was disappointed when they reunited during the winter and I was pulled from school so we could all move to Nebraska.

Not everyone could afford college for their kids, but given the interest shown by educators when I was thirteen, it seemed an injustice that my future was left to fate. Most families, like those in the front seat, would take notice and try to lend a partial assist. On our ride to Chicago, the people quizzed me about my experience at the university, but then drew us into an uneasy debate about the Vietnam draft versus our antiwar views. Their son sat in the front with them and didn't say much. I wondered if he agreed with us and didn't want to speak up, or if he disagreed with us and let his parents do the talking for him. After all, by keeping him in college they'd be ensuring his draft deferment, while too many other families would soon lose their boys for no good or rational reason. Just because I couldn't afford more college, I didn't intend to donate my life as an extra in Lyndon Johnson's war movie. If the government considered me expendable, they were misinformed. Lyndon Johnson was just an extra in *my* movie.

CHAPTER 6

In Chicago Joe and I sat down on the steps of an 'L' station to ponder, a little lost and helpless amid the indifferent commuters streaming past. I had no idea what to do next and felt sorry that I'd got us into this uncertain predicament. After a long while four or five guys and girls our age and looking sort of nonconformist like us came down the stairs and we traded friendly hellos. Joe and I sat there for another hour or so, and here came that same group again. This time they stopped and one of them noted the obvious.

"You guys still here?"

"Yeah," said Joe. "We haven't figured out where we're going."

"We just got into town, and don't know anybody," I said.

"You should come with us to Old Town."

"What's that?"

"A tourist area. You'll see."

It was a long, jerking ride on the elevated, with flashing lights, rattling couplings, rumbling wooden ties and wheels screeching on rails. They didn't have anything like it in Lincoln. Already Chicago was an adventure. We walked in the dark to a house on North Sedgwick, about three houses away from North Avenue, up some steps and across a covered porch. Inside there were more people, mostly about our age, some of them younger. One guy about twenty named Mario seemed to be most in charge.

There was no furniture and we sat down on the living room floor with them, leaning against the walls in a big circle, and regaled them with our hitchhiking tale. I pulled out a loaf of bread and asked if anybody wanted some. One or two took a slice, and Mario said they could make some spaghetti. Some of us migrated to the kitchen while the noodles boiled. When they were ready there was nothing to put on them except salt and pepper.

With a laugh Mario said, "Have some of our five-dollar salt and pepper."

"Oh yeah?" Joe asked. "Five dollars?" That sounded like about four dollars and ninety cents too much. I mean, look at the haul of groceries I'd bought for five dollars.

One of the girls said, "We got caught shoplifting them. So the store manager made us give him five dollars not to call the cops."

"He let you go?"

"Yeah, and he let us keep the salt and pepper."

I'd stolen a ready-made sandwich once, and some of my college books. A guy I knew in Lincoln had been arrested in the supermarket for slipping steaks under his jacket. The likelihood of getting caught was enough to keep me from stealing food more often.

They said we could stay there at Sedgwick if we wanted to. We sat around talking some more and I found out you could make some money for a day's work at a place called Add-a-Man. You showed up early in the morning and Add-a-Man sent you out to a one-day temporary job. The guys said it was hard work. I didn't mind working, I just didn't want to have to get a haircut, and they said Add-a-Man didn't care how you looked. That was a big difference from Lincoln.

The girls didn't work at Add-a-Man and neither would a lot of the guys. They told us they went to the 'L' stations downtown and asked for spare change from people who were on their way to work in the morning. I guess some people did give them money. Standing on the street and asking complete strangers for a handout was something I never would have done in Lincoln, never even thought of. It was a little frightening to contemplate.

We all crashed on the floor and the next day a couple of the guys took Joe and me to Add-a-Man. I was broke and looked forward to earning some cash. I got assigned to a group going to the Rawlins television factory, and Joe and my Sedgwick friends were sent other places. I was a little scared to be separated on my own. Another guy assigned to Rawlins said he could take five of us in his car. I thought he was taking us because he was a good guy and was going that way anyhow, but after we all got in he made us each cough up twenty-five cents to ride. I guessed it was just the dog-eat-dog nature of a city like Chicago. Luckily I had a quarter to give him, leaving me about twenty cents to my name.

I'd never heard of Rawlins TVs before. When we got there they led all the Add-a-Man people around and left us off in ones and twos. I was teamed up with a full-time worker, a good-natured black guy, maybe ten, fifteen years older than me who gave me some plastic goggles and work gloves. I noticed he was wearing thick-soled work boots, and all I had was my worn out old loafers over some socks with holes in them.

"So you're one of the Add-a-Man guys, huh?" he said.

"Yep."

"Where you live at?"

"I'm staying in Old Town with some people," I said, and decided to elaborate. "I just hitchhiked here yesterday."

"Hitchhiked from where?"

"Nebraska."

"Nebraska! Good grief. Okay now watch me. Here's what you do."

Our job was to lift the heavy television picture tubes from a suspended slow-moving conveyor and set them face up into a machine. It did some hocus-pocus to the back end of the tube when you stepped on a pedal, and then you lifted the picture tube back onto the conveyor. Pure repetitive labor, nothing mental involved.

We took turns pulling TV tubes off the conveyor. It was plain a string bean like me didn't have the upper body strength for continuous repeated lifting, but I gave it my best. The heat and humidity in Chicago wasn't exactly invigorating. My partner could see I was struggling to keep up. He could have griped about getting stuck with somebody almost useless, or yelled at me, only he was pretty cool. Sort of joking, he asked me what I had for breakfast.

"I didn't have breakfast," I said, lifting another picture tube off the conveyor. Going without meals had become a regular habit which I had to admit wasn't working too well. Much of the time I didn't have a choice.

"You mean you're running on empty."

"That's about it."

Knowing I was a temporary helper for the day, he must have begun to guess I was destitute, except maybe not as useless as some of the winos who dragged in from Add-a-Man. At the noon whistle he asked, "What're you doing about lunch?"

"Nothing I guess," I said.

I was surprised when he took a dollar out of his wallet. "Here. Get yourself something to eat."

He gave me directions to the plant cafeteria where I had the hot plate special and pie and a Coke. Afterwards I gave him his change and thanked him for the meal. My biggest impression of Rawlins was his thoughtful generosity. Blacks still got a pretty lousy deal in this country, no matter the new Civil Rights Act.

Back at Add-a-Man that afternoon I collected my day's pay. Maybe it was the guy's example that caused me to buy some groceries for the house at Sedgwick, and also gratitude for the spaghetti dinner. And I still had more money left over than I'd had in a while.

I'd started out with ambitions to make some money at Add-a-Man for a few days, but I was discouraged by the actuality. Like they had said, it wasn't good work and the pay was uninspiring, so most guys wouldn't go more than a day or two. Instead of working, I walked two blocks over to historic Old Town the next day and made some friends among the people hanging out on Wells Street. It was a tourist area of clubs and shops, not close enough to the university to include what you might consider an intellectual bunch.

The street crowd weren't students or poets like my friends in Lincoln. Some were a teenage and young twenties mixture who worked in the shops along North Wells Street and Maiden Lane and Pipers Alley, like the record store and the leather shop. Others were teenyboppers who rode in for the day on the 'L' train to get a taste of freedom, and panhandlers asking tourists for spare change, which I was reluctant to try myself. They were Chicago natives, from either the inner city or suburbs like Evanston and Skokie. They lived on the street during the day and stayed at crash pads or went home at night.

Billy Neighbor, Dirty Ralph, and Friendly Fred were some of the first friends I made. A scruffy chatterbox named Nick showed me how he was trying to jam pay phones and parking meters with a screwdriver so he could come back later and get the coins out. I believe he was more enthusiastic than he was successful. I watched him with curiosity, not very bothered about the illegal aspect. Chicago was a place where people took bribes from shoplifters, held you up for gas money, and sabotaged coin-operated machines. It was also a place where people let you crash, or would give you a dollar to eat.

Other regulars on Wells Street were the black shoeshine boys, pre-teenagers toting small wooden boxes of rags and polish and brushes, accosting everyone to offer them a shine. The boys asked me too, but my scuffed up old loafers, the ones I used to polish with such diligence in high school, had no need of a shine and I wasn't going to pay ten cents for it. Groups of the boys sometimes performed a military-style drill on the sidewalk, stepping in drum-and-bugle corps formation and chanting, "Blackstone Rangers, mighty mighty Rangers," drawing a small crowd of onlookers. I didn't know whether the Blackstone Rangers that the kids looked up to were a club or a criminal gang. Some people said they were both. Tourists tossed coins at the kids, who finished their routine and then scrambled to snatch up the money and disperse to find more shoeshine customers. I figured it was their city and they had more right to be there than all the idlers like myself. At least they did a service for their money.

Joe Knight decided to stay in Chicago for a while. I restocked my duffel bag with canned corn and stew and a loaf of bread and set out for Cleveland, 350 miles away, to look for d. a. levy. I was a little uneasy, since I'd only actually hitchhiked to Omaha, and with Joe for company, and we had come the rest of the way by bus or with the Grinnell family. East of the city a steady flow of truck traffic was going to places like Gary and Detroit, and I soon caught a ride.

In Cleveland I studied street maps on gas station walls, boarded city buses, and asked directions as I got close enough to walk. Someone on the street pointed and told me, "Go two blocks that way to the Piggly-Wiggly and turn left one block." I would have telephoned first, if anybody could afford to have a phone back then. Instead I knocked at d. a. levy's door with no prior notice, the same way I'd appeared at Matt Shulman's door.

Levy was five or six years older than me, pale and diminutive, with a short scraggly beard. He wore buckled motorcycle boots, blue jeans, and a light brown military surplus shirt.[1] I wasn't as dazzled as I thought I'd be. He was even less impressive than Matt Shulman and seemed a little suspicious until I said Matt had sent me. It intrigued him that someone had made a pilgrimage to seek him out. It wasn't every day that a kid showed up at his door and said, "Hey man, I heard about you and hitchhiked 800 miles to talk about poetry." If he thought the Cleveland poetry movement was remote from New York, then here, in the form of myself, was a manifestation from still deeper in the uncultured wilds of the continental outback.

He lived with his Latvian girlfriend Dagmar, who was a year younger than me. I wouldn't have heard of Latvia except by coincidence some Latvians went to my high school in Lincoln. I offered some of my canned food for dinner and Levy was appalled that I had lugged the heavy groceries. While we opened stew and warmed the contents he advised me to travel lighter in the future, and recounted his own experience hitchhiking to California and back. I gave him a copy of my book of poems and asked if he could let me crash on his floor. He said for two nights only, long enough to find somewhere else to stay.

Next morning he leafed through my book and showed me a few of his mimeographed publications, including *Marrahwannah Quarterly*. His printings were a lot more creative and visual than the book I'd made. I'd only been exposed to the university-sanctioned *Scrip*, and when I printed my own poems I thought it was an original idea. Here in Cleveland was the real mimeo revolution—the one that I'd been missing out on in Nebraska.

In those days before photocopiers, the poetry pamphlets cranked out on letterpress or mimeograph machines were an underground art form sort of like street theater or garage bands. During my school years, there'd been mimeo handouts in class, the kind with smudged purple lettering on damp paper smelling of ink. By the sixties, mimeograph use was widespread and the print quality had improved. The ordinary copier was still in the future.

Levy wrote both outrageous rants and genuinely good poetry. He not only wrote and illustrated, he was an epicenter of poetic activity. I didn't yet realize that he'd been publishing his own as well as other people's poetry for over three years already, including notables like Ed Sanders and Charles Bukowski. Some was work by local poets who wrote commentaries on regional issues such as the pollution of Lake Erie and the Cuyahoga River. By the time I met him, he'd put together nearly a hundred publications.[2]

In the afternoon he suggested that the three of us go out for a drink. I was pleased to find out that in Ohio eighteen-year-olds could have 3.2 beer. Better than nothing. I wasn't old enough to have real beer but I was old enough to be shipped to Vietnam to have my real butt blown away. Great place, America.

While we walked to a bar some people speeding by in a dark brown humpbacked sedan from the forties honked and yelled at us. They were tooting at Levy because of his beard, and at me for having longish hair like the Beatles, still a novelty then outside of cities like San Francisco and New York. Levy scowled and shook his fist, gave them some obscene sign in anger. At the same time I blew them a kiss. It was a response I'd developed for when I was harassed by intolerant bigots and similar honkeys. (That's a joke about horn-honking and honkeys. In the Sixties, "honkey" was a derogatory term blacks used to describe racist whites.)

Levy said, "Hey, that's pretty cool. I'm gonna do that too." He saw the Zen coolness of it, the opposite of an angry reaction, as if loving thine enemy was a better retort than returning their insult. He blew a kiss to try it out, although the car was a block away by then. In this way, I think we had a fair trade, where I brought him a little enlightenment. It was kindred to Allen Ginsberg's handshake with a cloud, a little touch of higher consciousness. Maybe I was a good influence on Levy without realizing it, and he repaid me later by taking me to poetry readings and printing some of my poems.

Levy helped me find another place to stay, at Diane and Phil's apartment. "Phil" was short for Phyllis. Both girls worked and made their living room floor available to itinerants who needed a place to crash. Over the next day or two I was either out visiting d. a. levy or meeting more of the population that was constantly dropping in at Diane's. Just about everyone was a lot less broke than me.

One couple who was crashing there showed up with a jug of red wine and Bob Dylan's brand new double album *Blonde on Blonde*. I told them that Dylan and the Hawks had played a one-night concert in Lincoln less than three months earlier, soon after Allen Ginsberg's visit. We'd all gone together—me, Darlene, Grady, Rich Johnston, Joe Knight, and the rest of our group. Darlene had been miffed at me and said I was disrespectful, because during the concert I wrote a poem about it.

On the new album I recognized one of the songs he had played at his concert, "Leopard-skin Pillbox Hat." We sat on the living room floor, just the three of us, slouched against the walls and drinking wine, listening closely to *Blonde on Blonde* two or three times. It took over an hour to play all four sides. The next day they shared another jug of wine and we played the album again a couple of times. By then I knew some of the lyrics pretty well.

When I left Lincoln, I hadn't known how long I would be away. Now I felt an obligation to get back and finish up classes, in case I'd be able to continue as a sophomore in the fall. My new *Blonde on Blonde* friends were driving to St. Louis, which was sort of in the right direction, westward, and they brought me along. They knew a place where I could stay overnight and by evening we ended up in Gaslight Square, a night club district.

They left me with their friends, two guys in an upstairs apartment that overlooked the decorative lamp posts and tourist crowds below who were prowling the street. One of the guys rolled a joint that they shared with me. The other sat in an armchair beneath a floor lamp in a corner, patiently stuffing gelatin capsules with white powder to sell —mescaline or something. He offered me some but I didn't want to try it. I slept on the couch and in the morning thanked them and went out.

I thought my dad was at Scott Air Force Base outside of East St. Louis. We had lived there two different times when I was a kid. I knew he was back in the states now, temporarily at Scott after his tour in the Azores, and I sort of had the idea to look him up. I didn't have an actual phone number and when I tried calling the base, they didn't have any information on where to find him.

I was still timid about hitchhiking as a way to get five hundred miles back to Lincoln. I started asking people on the sidewalk for spare change, so I could buy a bus ticket, and met a girl who offered to bring me to a college campus where she was a student. She said some of her friends might help me. In the student lounge they gathered around a table and I told my story and tried to take up a collection. Some pitched in small change, and after about two hours I had nowhere near enough for a bus ticket. The girl ended up loaning me ten dollars and I got her address so I could pay her back later.

The overnight bus got me to Lincoln and I walked to my place. When the manager heard me come in he opened his door to tell me that my parents had been by while I was away. What flawless timing.

CHAPTER 7

I hadn't seen my parents in over a year and had no reason to expect they were coming. Whatever were they doing five hundred miles from St. Louis and six hundred miles from northern Wisconsin? I didn't think it was due to a sudden interest in my education, like the family I met in Grinnell. There could have been some business at Lincoln Air Force Base regarding my dad's military discharge, because they would not have driven twenty or more hours roundtrip just to visit me. I pictured them cruising into town in their floating boat of a luxury car. It would be unprecedented for them to pop in with a we're-here-for-you-son announcement, as if they had a stake in whether I went to college or not.

Bob said they had asked to see my room, but he wouldn't unlock it for them. I was relieved that he respected my privacy and was glad I hadn't been there when they came. I used Steve Abbott's phone to call them person-to-person collect. The old man was piqued that I hadn't been there to swoop in and ambush like some sitting duck. I made up a plausible story on the spot, that I'd been meeting a publisher in Omaha. I didn't mention Cleveland, though I embellished the truth by adding I'd gone to St. Louis to look for him. I explained about the girl who had loaned me bus fare and persuaded him to send me an extra ten dollars, which I mailed to her.

. . .

Professor Hilliard welcomed my return to English Lit and listened to me describe where I'd been for the previous week and a half. Starting out for Omaha was understandable enough. Adding a detour through Chicago, Cleveland, and St. Louis was either bold or foolhardy.

He returned a stack of poems that I had left with him to look over. With a kind manner he said, "I read some of these to the class."

"Oh." I was afraid to ask him which ones or what the class thought of them, if anything. Were there any who didn't scratch their heads at those awful poems? Were they uncomprehending, like the student at Kearney who asked me if I felt like I accomplished something?

"Gee," was all I could say.

"Sorry about the coffee ring on the front," he said to me. "It isn't mine. I loaned them to Karl Shapiro and that's his coffee." Other than using them to set his coffee on though, I don't know what Karl thought of them, or if he even looked at them. I'm sure they were no less clumsy and no more interesting than other student work. It was funny, a private joke to me, that Karl Shapiro didn't know I was the same person who interviewed him at his home, or who had hosted the big party for him and Allen Ginsberg. Or maybe—if he remembered mentioning my book in the campus newspaper article he wrote in April—well maybe he did recognize my name.

I must have exemplified my professor's view of a true poetic soul, because for the semester he gave me an A. It was another instance when the outside world conferred me with acceptance, in direct contradiction to my family environment.

I resumed my university classes for the remaining couple of weeks and took final exams. It was a formality, my habit of finishing things I started. I'd kept up the high marks needed to maintain a student exemption. Guys whose grades fell below a certain threshold lost their 2-S student deferment and could be drafted by the army. Without money though, I wouldn't be attending a second year and would lose the 2-S status. I didn't have a prospect of getting work that paid enough to keep me going beyond rent and subsistence living, so saving up my own money for tuition was impossible. It never occurred to me to seek another student loan, or that my friends took out loans with help from their families. I assumed they all got money from home to live on, and had their university expenses covered. They had not heard the words, "If you want to go to college I'll pay your rent, but you have to pay for everything else yourself."

So now, a year and a half after leaving home, I was on the run again. This time going AWOL not from family but from Lincoln and the impossibility of college. I had to try to evade the reach of the Vietnam draft, euphemistically known as the Selective Service System. I was determined not to be selected and not to serve, and not to be swallowed up by somebody else's so-called system. Darlene's desertion hadn't helped my morale. It was all piling up on me. After four years on the prairie I still wasn't calling myself a Nebraska resident. I was about done with my Lincoln Bardo.

Bob was cool about me giving up my room. I had a few boxes of belongings and books and my typewriter that I stored in the basement, to come back and get when I wanted. I should have had the sense to foresee that he would leave too and naturally take the typewriter. He and his wife had been kind to me though, lowering the rent when I'd moved in so I could afford it, and turning me on to weed.

I left behind all my issues of *Scrip*, including the one containing my poem about Ginsberg, and the "Auto Poesy to Nebraska" insert, intending to retrieve them later but never doing so. With my blanket and duffel bag lightly packed—no canned food this time—I ventured out to mingle with leading-edge poets instead of academic ones. In the guise of a poet I was foremost a seeker, not of a city of gold or a fountain of youth, but a grail, holy or otherwise, the last lost knight of the Round Table ranging improbably far.

. . .

Matt Shulman had finished printing his first issue of *Do-It!*. He gave me two copies when I stopped in Omaha to see him for the second time, on my way to Cleveland. The yellow paper cover had an illustration by d. a. levy and listed poetry by Levy himself, Allen Ginsberg (deliberately misspelled Ginsburg for some sort of copyright reason, Matt said), Clarence Major, Freda Norton, Matt Shulman, and wow—Randy Rhody. There were additional poets inside, and I was honored to see my name on the front cover. Price was fifty cents. Yeah, if that kid at Kearney State College asked me now, I felt like I'd accomplished something.

I wasn't in *Do-It!* because my reputation had grown equal to Ginsberg's. He was so omnipresent that our paths crossed a few times that year. His poem was the very same one that the English Department chairman had barred from *Scrip* two months earlier. "Auto Poesy to Nebraska" survives to this day. Holding onto things wasn't something I did well in those tumbleweed times and I lost my copies of *Do-It!* very quickly.[1]

In Chicago I stopped long enough to earn a day's pay at Add-a-Man, where they sent me to the Rawlins television factory again. I slept at North Sedgwick and pushed on to Cleveland. When I got there I went to Diane and Phil's first, to make sure I could crash there again, and then went to find d. a. levy. He'd already seen *Do-It!* with both our names on the cover.

That evening he and I walked to a storefront coffee house called The Well, a community-sponsored hangout for teenagers. At scattered tables inside were about a dozen kids having coffee or sodas. We took a vacant table by the window and Levy stood up and called for everyone's attention, and introduced me as a traveling poet just arrived from Chicago. I stood next to my chair and read some of my poems for about ten minutes. There was a bit of applause after each one. Not counting the times I had read at the Hyde Park gatherings in Lincoln, The Well was my second public reading after my appearance at Kearney State.

Instead of passing around a collection basket, Levy stood again to remind patrons to make a contribution to the poet. To my surprise one guy about my age came over, enthusiastic about my reading, and gave me two quarters—enough to buy a burger, fries, and a Coke at McDonald's. A couple others brought me a dime, fifteen cents. Poets like us didn't stay in it for the money.

Maybe Levy respected my willingness to do the spontaneous reading, so much like guerrilla street theater. Sort of an initiation. After *Do-It!* I was hopeful to be published again and Levy looked through all my poems and picked five to put together in a printing. He proposed an edition of 125 copies, which amounted to a lot of printing supplies. I agreed to pay for the needed paper and he would supply the stencils and ink.

I went along and watched him at his mimeo setup in Adelaide Simon's basement. She was a long-time poet and playwright whose husband Martin played cello with the Cleveland Symphony. Levy kept his equipment at their house instead of at his apartment so that whenever he moved he'd still have his press in a permanent location. He was also paranoid that the police would raid his apartment and wreck or confiscate his equipment. They were harassing him at the time for printing what they considered obscene material. That is to say, naughty words like Allen Ginsberg used. Being off on my own mystical journey, I just wasn't into obscenity, which had nothing to do with the poetry I intended to write. Lao Tzu and Ezra Pound hadn't earned their reputations by using obscenities.

I wanted to call the collection *Paracutes*, for my own obscure reasons, because I was inventing words at that time. It also sounded somewhat Latin and scholarly. Others referred to it mistakenly as "Parachutes," but neither Levy nor I were careless enough to misspell words by accident. *Marrahwannah Quarterly* wasn't a misspelling.

For his regular publications, Levy took in submitted material and wrote a lot of the content himself. He used several press names, most commonly Renegade Press and Seven Flowers Press. This instance more resembled a writer-publisher relationship, with my work printed stand-alone rather than for a magazine. He printed it under the banner of 400 Rabbit Press, 400 Rabbits being something from Aztec mythology about drunken rabbits that I hadn't heard about before.

After the printing he and Dagmar and I sat in the sunlight on their bare wooden floor and Levy directed the assembly process. He collated the pages and stapled each booklet together. Dagmar finger painted the covers, each one unique, and laid them out on the floor to dry. When they were ready I glued a cover painting onto the front of each book. In *Paracutes* she is credited with the artwork. For publications, Levy shuffled some letters of Dagmar's name into MaRa, the Ra part making an Egyptian sort of alias. At the same time, MaRa resembled the "Marrah" part of Marrahwannah. Levy and I each took half of the finished copies, him to list for sale in *Marrahwannah Quarterly*, and me to give away or sell for spare change. I sent one to Professor Hilliard in Lincoln.

The little book of five poems would eventually come to rest in the special collections and rare book archives of at least three universities, with its own WorldCat OCLC number.[2] If I'd known I was writing rare books, I would have written more.

There was one poem out of those five that I liked most, titled "Underworld Odyssey." It suited me to use rhyme, and it wasn't political. The theme was mainly philosophical or existential, reminiscent of hitchhiking and wandering.

> *we'll wander*
> *around the world*
> *on rainy days*
>
> *and squander*
> *spinning time*
> *in a non-stop maze*

nowhereing
to unlocated
silent corners of gardens

uncaring
for epithets
or welcomes or pardons

we'll blend
like fading smoke
in a phosphorescent light

to the end
on a voyage
to the bottom of the night

Levy's involvement had made the Cleveland poetry scene a vibrant place, far beyond anything in Lincoln. Much like Steve Abbott had been in Lincoln, he was something of a mentor and included me in his literary activities during the next few days. He took me to the Asphodel Book Shop and introduced me to the owner, Jim Lowell. The bookstore was located in a large old industrial building that had been repurposed as an assemblage of small shops. Besides mainstream books, Asphodel stocked small underground publications like Levy's *Marrahwannah Quarterly* and later *The Buddhist Third Class Junkmail Oracle,* and Levy left some copies of *Paracutes* to put on the shelves.

It seemed like a lot of writers weren't writing poetry as much as trying to draw attention. Many of the poems heard at public readings and that d. a. levy printed included profanity and phrases calculated for shock value, such as naming his magazine *Marrahwannah Quarterly*. He could have called his magazine *Cleveland Quarterly* or *Lake Erie Quarterly*, or anything else Quarterly. He had a way of making his own particular shocking poetry simultaneously humorous, sometimes so absurd I had to laugh.

To their credit, poets were also breaking the formal boundaries imposed on them by a previous establishment. Defiance of tradition had always been around. Rules were made to be broken, in particular establishment rules that demanded conformity. Conformity was one step away from oppression. Anyone who didn't conform was a threat to the established order, even in the innocent field of poetry.

Levy introduced me to the term "concrete poetry" and showed me some examples. They were a level beyond my "diagrammed sentences" poetry. Often the font was oversized, or laid out crooked. In fact, sometimes it looked like graffiti painted on walls and concrete sidewalks, and at first I thought that's how it got the name "concrete."

It was the poetic equivalent of electronic music and abstract art. It was interesting to look at but wasn't really to be read out loud. It was more like exercises in typesetting, because sometimes the interpretation depended on the appearance of the poem on a page.

I didn't try to imitate it because I was searching for my own style, and it looked to me like a lot of writers were copying each other. For instance, they adopted a lazy pattern of spelling "you" as "u" and "are" as "r", as would become commonplace on the internet decades later. But my own opinion was that this in itself didn't make something any more poetic or literary.

Three and a half months after our party for Allen Ginsberg in Lincoln, Ginsberg was coming to Cleveland to give a poetry reading at the university. Levy said it was for students and faculty only, or some such restriction, and I wouldn't be allowed to attend. As far as I knew Ginsberg only wrote poetry and didn't print material through a press of his own. Levy ran a bigger risk, eventually drawing police attention. Levy neglected to mention that he knew Ginsberg personally.[3] I could've schemed to go anyway, found Ginsberg and reminded him about Lincoln, and gotten permission to attend as his guest, but I didn't. It was probably not so different from the readings he'd done in Lincoln, except on this trip Peter and Julius Orlovsky weren't along.

The party for Ginsberg after his reading was a better opportunity anyway and I was able to go to that. It was at a posh home with parquet floors and polished wood, a more civilized venue than my apartment in Lincoln. This time he wasn't ensconced out of reach as he'd been at our party. It was my chance to kind of interview him one-on-one as I had interviewed Karl Shapiro in high school. When I saw Allen I shyly approached to shake his hand. This time he didn't stroke my palm. He didn't say that I shook hands with a cloud, either. He was holding a glass of beer and looked the same as he had in February, even looked to be wearing the same clothes.

"Do you remember me?" I asked.

"No," he answered.

I felt timid and foolish, not much braver than the cowardly lion when he met the wizard of Oz. Any normal person would have said to Allen, "Good to see you again. That was my place in Lincoln where we had the party for you and Karl Shapiro." I would tell him how his poem and my book had both been censored in Lincoln.

"Ah, sure, I remember you now," Ginsberg would say. "Then you must know Steve Abbott."

"We're good friends," I'd say. I would hand him a copy of *Paracutes.* "You and I both know d. a. levy too, of course."

"Oh, so you're a friend of Levy?"

"Yeah. Hey—you, me and Levy all had our poems printed in *Do-It!.*"

He probably knew Clarence Major. By this time Ginsberg would say, "You're in Matt Shulman's magazine too? Say, have you been to the Peace Eye Bookstore in New York? No? Come out sometime and look me up. I'll introduce you to Ed Sanders and Tuli Kupferberg."

Though it wouldn't have directly improved my writing ability, it was an opportunity for a kind of apprenticeship and reception into the guild of poets. Except we didn't have that fictional conversation because I failed to mention Lincoln. For a poet, I was severely tongue-tied. The same boldness that made me seek out Matt Shulman and d. a. levy evaporated in the awesome presence of Allen Ginsberg. Maybe the difference in our years kept me from speaking further, and a fear he might make a pass at me again. It was also a weird form of self-assurance. To prove myself worthy, I wanted to sink or swim on my own merit, not because of who I knew. Other poets would read my words and know me first by reputation. I was so used to going it alone that even where outsiders were assembled, I managed to shut myself out.

So, "Do you remember me?"

"No," he answered.

"Oh." End of conversation.

CHAPTER 8

B etween the two cities it was only a day's hitchhike, 350 miles, and I ricocheted back and forth. I preferred Cleveland and the educated crowd of aspiring poets I had discovered there. Call the Chicago-bound direction my commute to work, where whenever I needed a few dollars I worked a day for Add-a-Man. If I was frugal, it was enough to eat something most days, even if only a can of beans. I'll not exaggerate my labors however. In all of that year I made a tenth of what I'd made the previous year when I had the part-time delivery job.

I got into Chicago at night and headed to the crash pad on North Sedgwick. Compared to my first visit there, it was getting to be crowded with sleeping bodies. In any place that was wall-to-wall people at night, the kitchen might be the last to be claimed, and sometimes that's where I landed. I reasoned the floor was as clean as anywhere else since nobody actually cooked or ate there, and linoleum was softer than the wood floors in the other rooms. Besides which, I liked the idea of a roof over my head, even if it was a table instead of a tent, because nobody would step on me by accident.

A guy I didn't recognize was already under the table and I crouched down to glower at him. "You're in my spot," I said, and when he squirmed and began to apologize I grinned to let him know I was putting him on.

"If you could see yourself, man," I said, laughing. There was room for two so I asked, "Mind if I share this space?"

He smiled and shifted over for me.

I said, "Name's Randy."

"Hi. I'm Jim. Jim Craig." His thick glossy hair hung down just to his collar. The plaid short-sleeved shirt and dirty white jeans he wore seemed too small for him, like he'd outgrown them.

"You from Chicago?"

"No, Canada. Wawee, Ontario."

I said I'd just come back from Cleveland, and fished out a copy of *Paracutes*. He looked through the mimeoed booklet of my five poems with interest. During the following days I'd see him around on Wells Street and we got to be friends, as well as occasional bunkmates under the table.

Why didn't I tout d. a. levy's publication of my poems on the Wells Street sidewalk, holding up MaRa's finger-painted cover as people walked by?

"Poetry here," I called. "Original poems."

"How much?" someone asked.

"Twenty-five cents." Forget twenty-five cents. Dressed to look more like a poet, I could charge thirty-five cents each.

"Is this your poetry, young man?"

"Yep. And that's original artwork on each cover."

Surely many of the bored, curious, or culture-starved tourists that came would have bought souvenir copies.

"Here, I'll take two, if you'll autograph them."

"With pleasure," I said.

Except that never happened. Too bad. The novelty would have made d. a. levy and me profitable. Prosperous. Wealthy. So un-American of me not to keep my eye on the dollar. The dream of making art inspired me, but the prospect of merchandising it was intimidating.

. . .

Instead, as I strolled Wells Street one night with the other denizens I'd become friends with, a cop stole up from behind and singled me out of the sidewalk swarm. He didn't offer a reason for detaining me. I believe it was on suspicion of having long hair. I didn't know if he could do that, but I cooperated, since there wasn't any civil liberties lawyer around to intervene. It was frightening and unexpected, to be locked in the back seat of the blue and white patrol car while the cop went to capture another victim. It was a harassment technique to round up consistent loiterers who obviously weren't in Old Town to spend money and enrich the merchants. I suppose the dragnet tactic might snare anyone carrying a contraband substance. I knew a lot of people who could get grass or pills, but nobody'd be dumb enough to be holding.

After a time a paddy wagon arrived and I was handcuffed and loaded in through the back doors, to sit with half a dozen black, Hispanic, and white youths. Nobody looked especially dangerous or criminal, and all were stoic and silent on the ride, during which the wagon stopped a couple more times to load in other offenders. At a precinct station we were frisked and locked up for the night with more prisoners. We weren't officially booked with fingerprints and mug shots. The night's routine mass roundup would be sorted out later to see who they'd keep and who they'd throw back. I was paired in a cell with a thirty-something Hispanic man who looked decent enough, dressed neatly in slacks and a white shirt and navy sweater, not drunk or violent.

The lights stayed on all night and breakfast was served at daybreak—watery coffee and a thin slice of bologna between two slices of Wonder Bread. They forgot the mayonnaise, lettuce, and tomato, with pickle and chips on the side. Most prisoners in the nearby cells yelled at the guards and tossed their dry sandwiches into the corridor. I devoured mine. It was the same unembellished food I normally ate. My cell mate threw his sandwich too, and then when he saw how hungry I was, he said, "Oh, sorry. I would have given you mine."

His considerate remark surprised me. "It's okay. Thanks anyhow," I said.

After our morning repast we were loaded into a van and transferred to another jail, which turned out to be at the Cook County courthouse, and staged in a large communal cell, then herded to a courtroom in groups and one at a time stood before a judge. I didn't know what the charge was, something spurious, I guessed, like loitering. I was braced for some harsh interrogation.

"How do you like it back there?" the judge said.

"What?" I didn't know what he meant.

"Back there in the cell. You like it there?"

"No sir."

Then he asked me what I did. *This year I published some poems in Do-It! and a booklet named Paracutes. Oh, and my book A Year's Worth of Wonder.* Yeah, right. I didn't think mentioning poetry would make a big impression just then. I shed my artist persona and donned the bourgeois semblance of a well-behaved drudge.

"I work part time," I said, which technically I did, at Add-a-Man. "And I'll be at the University of Wisconsin in Madison this fall." I was still under the delusion that I might be able to raise tuition somehow.

He seemed to drop the hard attitude and became fairly casual with me.

"What's your major?"

"English and anthropology."

"English and anthropology," he mused aloud, then dismissed me. I walked back to Old Town.

Dirty Ralph and I sauntered past a Wells Street parking lot where a family of four was getting out of their car. The two smiling daughters who looked to be in their early teens hailed us.

"Hey, can we take your picture?"

"Sure." I was flattered. They produced a Polaroid camera and we slouched against a brick wall and tried to look bohemian for them—bored, aloof, and authentic. We waited while the picture developed so we could see how it looked.

If anything, we were part of the attraction to Old Town. It shows how out of touch the cops were by harassing us. They should have welcomed us. The merchants should have paid us. We were a new phenomenon, part of what tourists came to see. There wasn't much remarkable about our appearance, wearing the clothes we slept in, except we were the first wave to let our hair grow blatantly uncut, when the length of a guy's hair really mattered. It was a declaration of independence and defiance of the System, not a fashion affectation. Long hair identified us as freedom fighters and outlaws. Like a badge of rank, the longer it was proved how long we'd been with the Resistance.

"Can you take another one for us to keep?" I asked and they did. Later I taped it into the notebook I always carried.

When I was ready to head east again I asked Jim the Canadian if he was interested in going along to New York by way of Cleveland. First I wanted to earn some travel money, so we both worked for Add-a-Man for a couple of days before setting out. At the Rawlins plant Jim and I were teamed up lifting television tubes from a conveyor and packing them into sturdy cardboard cartons that we assembled on shipping pallets. A forklift operator would come and take the completed pallets, to be trucked to another location, where they'd be put into finished cabinets with more electronics and speakers.

"Where's that guy with the forklift?" He hadn't been by in a while and our area was too crowded now to put down a fresh pallet.

"Beats me," I said. I loaded another picture tube into the carton.

"There's room for three more in this one, and that's it," Jim reminded me.

Nobody had said the picture tubes would keep circling around the plant on the conveyor if we let them go by the first time. We were under the impression that we had only one chance to unload them.

They had a thin glass spike that extended from the back and we'd been told if the spike was broken we should leave the tube on the conveyor.

"Well, some of these are broken," I said to Jim. "Look." I snapped off the back of a perfectly intact picture tube.

Jim giggled. "It's true," he said, and broke the next one. Finally the forklift came, but when it was too slow, we broke more tubes as they went past us. If they were broken, somebody further down the line couldn't accuse us of letting ready-to-ship tubes go by uncollected.

Ironic that we labored in a television factory. Nobody I knew owned a TV. Our truth came out of the songs on radio and record players.

When we each had two or three days' pay, enough to last for weeks, Jim and I headed east at night. Outside of Gary, Indiana a box truck slowed and pulled onto the shoulder. We ran up to open the passenger door and the driver said, "How far you going?"

"Cleveland."

"I'm going to Detroit with a delivery, and after that back down to the highway by Toledo," he said. "I can take you if you help me unload in the morning."

"Yeah sure, okay." At Toledo we'd be about a hundred miles from Cleveland.

"There's only room in front for one of you, so the other has to ride in the back."

His freight was unrefrigerated orange juice in metal crates. We flipped a coin and Jim got locked in with the cargo for five hours, trying to lay on the tops of bottles sticking into his ribs, a poor imitation of a swami on a bed of nails. Up front I mostly dozed.

In Detroit it was already hot, with the sun just up. We worked in the back of the truck, shoving crates down a metal roller ramp to where the driver and a man on the loading dock stacked them. The trucker chided us in a good-natured way about being slowpokes. He wanted to get back on the highway to his next delivery. After we finished he gave us each a bottle of warm orange juice to drink. He took us south out of Michigan to the main east-west route and this time it was my turn to ride in the back. It was a shorter trip and now that some of the crates were gone I could sit on the floor.

With Toledo behind us, Jim and I continued on to Cleveland. About midday we took a break and napped out of sight in a corn field. Later I found a piece of corrugated cardboard by the road and started to write CLEAVE LAND on it—two words. It wasn't finished when I held up my sign for an approaching car, and an old man and a little girl stopped to give us a ride. The man acknowledged my poet's joke about cleaving the land, and said his granddaughter had urged him to stop for us.

CHAPTER 9

I t was the first of July, a Friday evening. The next in a series of open-mic poetry readings that d. a. levy had helped organize was taking place at The Gate. It was a coffee house for students located in the basement of Trinity Cathedral at Cleveland State University, a few miles from the Adele's neighborhood. Levy and several of us took the bus there. Through a side gate in a wrought-iron fence, for which The Gate was named, we went down a stairway and entered a basement room with a coffee bar and subdued lighting. A podium in front held a Chianti wine bottle with a burning candle in it to lend a bit of atmosphere. Doesn't everyone read poetry by candle light?

We each put our name on a list to read up to three of our original poems to the audience. By the time the first reader began, all tables and chairs were taken and there was standing room only. I knew from my experience reading at Kearney State and at The Well that I'd be able to force my nervousness aside when it was my turn. To look as flamboyant as possible, I'd washed and combed my hair to dramatize its length, and put on the most colorful clothes I had, including a red sweater in spite of the heat.

On stage I removed my glasses, again for the sake of appearance, and read my three poems, including one from the *Paracutes* booklet. A camera flash went off while I was reading and when I finished and sat down a young reporter from the Cleveland *Plain Dealer* came over. She asked to copy the untitled poem from *Paracutes*. I showed it to her, not expecting that it would actually end up in the newspaper.

> throw your suitcases out in the rain
> then hurry like nonsense and vanish
> into the night
> run faster, faster until you're free
> where you can be simply
> whatever you choose
> they say you are lost
> but what they really mean is now they can't bury you
> children take care of yourselves
> and darken all the grinning time keepers
> with their backs to the rainbows

I assumed after she sorted out her complete notes and went through them to write her story she'd have plenty of good stuff and wouldn't need mine. In fact my poem and photograph would appear in a Cleveland *Plain Dealer* story about the gathering. My earlier pains to look noticeable must have worked.

I should have asked her for spare change or a meal. Talked her into chauffeuring me around. I was naïve though, not your ordinary conniving opportunist, nor a romanticized Hollywood version of a poet. Genuine poets are seers too saintly to scheme for their own advantage. Not always as calculating as establishment academics will have you believe, with analyses and interpretations, perspectives and postmortems. They walk absent-mindedly on clouds without caring if anyone notices.

Levy collected poems from the reading into *Poets At The Gate Vol. 1, No. 4.*[1] His publishing example was infectious. Samples of my poetry appeared in several Cleveland-related small press issues. After The Gate reading Carl Woidek asked if he could use one of my poems for a collection he wanted to print, called *Sum.* Other aspiring publishers would ask if they could use a poem and I always said yes.

Usually they sent me a copy or two, if they had an address for me, or gave me copies if I was in town at the time. Usually I lost them.

That Ohio enclave was remarkable in its vitality, as were likely many clusters of writers and artists across the nation. But while New York and California glorified their own creatives, outliers were neglected, ultimately erased from history. If Levy had moved to New York, he would have been immortalized.

Adele's Lounge Bar on Euclid Avenue was one of the reasons I felt more at home in Cleveland than in Chicago. At eighteen I could legally drink Schaefer's, the low-alcohol beer brewed in Cleveland. A fringe benefit was that I met a lot of people there and could ask around and find a place to stay overnight, some crash pad with floor space not already filled to capacity. It was near Case Western Reserve University, catering to a mixed crowd of university folk, poets, beatniks, and bikers.

The outlaw bikers in their sleeveless denim jackets were a local area club, not Hells Angels but just as menacing when they wanted to be, and staked out their own tables at Adele's. They weren't overly convivial, though not there to disturb the peace or make anyone else uneasy. They were part of the scene, their chrome-covered choppers parked rear wheel to the curb in a row directly in front of Adele's door, seeming to have permanently reserved that spot. Once in a while a cluster of bikers would exit the bar together and kick start their machines with an exhibitionist uproar, and then blast down Euclid Avenue in a magnificent pack. I knew motorcycles weren't for me even if I had the money for one. If I started riding, sooner or later I'd break my neck.

I spent time in Adele's and other places with a strawberry blonde named Bev. She didn't crash at Diane's with us but lived with her parents in well-to-do Shaker Heights. I think she'd just graduated high school. I was awestruck and wondered what she saw in the likes of me. I guess she wanted to walk on the wild side and after all I was a bohemian poet. One night when Adele's was packed, Bev and I shared a table with a sport-coated grad-student sort. I traded him one of my poetry booklets for a beer.[2]

Bev didn't share my disdain for the System, and thought I should cut my hair and find a job, be her boyfriend. She didn't know how like a hunted animal I felt, how I tried to be a moving target that the draft might ignore, even though I knew it was wishful thinking. But I figured if I cut my hair and got a job like an obedient and well-behaved peasant, they would seize me all the quicker and send me to Vietnam, at which time Bev would find a new boyfriend and mail me a Dear John letter. I couldn't see myself acting out that script.

The Simons, Adelaide and Martin, the ones who harbored Levy's printing press in their basement, had a daughter Celeste who hung out with the same crowd as I did. She was my age, but her parents were somewhat older than mine, and nicer. I thought it must be great to have artistic parents. The family took Jim and me to see the Fourth of July fireworks celebration. It reminded me of the fatal fireworks raining down on guys my age halfway around the world, both American and Vietnamese. I was feeling a diminished enthusiasm for the rocket's red glare and bombs bursting in air. My taste ran more to the rustle of a breeze in the tops of the trees.

Afterwards, the Simons gave us a ride out to the highway where we wanted to be dropped off so we could hitchhike to New York. Jim and I must have looked frail and improbable, two empty-handed kids coolly saying, "Oh sure, abandon us like unwanted puppies in the ditch. We'll just pop over to New York, five hundred miles or so, no big deal."

When Mr. Simon pulled over to let us out, he asked if we had any money. We'd pretty much used our Add-a-Man pay by then. I answered that we had a couple of dollars. He reached for his wallet and took out a five-dollar bill, a generous amount, and handed it to me in the back seat. I was reluctant to take it but the money would get us something to eat along the way, so I thanked him and accepted it. We got out and waved a last goodbye.

PART III

DRIFTING

CHAPTER 10

By early morning we found ourselves walking through the green fields and trees of Pennsylvania, a low mist hovering over the ground. The peaceful scene was a contrast to the previous night's fireworks. A trucker who was going to Washington D.C. stopped for us. I guessed we'd at least be on the east coast, bound to catch a ride going north to New York. Without a map, I didn't realize what a major detour going through West Virginia and Maryland was.

That night found us walking north out of Washington toward Baltimore, not yet twenty-four hours after we had left Cleveland. We hadn't been dropped on the main highway and were hitchhiking on a pretty dark stretch of local truck route. I put my thumb out for a pair of headlights and too late saw the unlit police light on its roof. A state trooper pulled alongside us and the passenger window slid down.

I was apprehensive, in the habit of bracing for trouble whenever I encountered The Law. I expected the uniformed officer to ask for our ID and what we were doing. Instead, without getting out of his car, he broke the silence. "Well? Do you need a ride?"

That surprised me. "Yeah, thanks." I got in front and Jim got in back.

"I can take you a few miles before I have to turn around."

"Sure, thanks. Any little distance is good." He was giving us a ride, no questions asked. Wow. For a cop that was pretty cool. Not like Chicago, for sure.

As we sped north he said, "If you boys want a place to stay overnight, there's a little police station up ahead I can take you to." It didn't seem like he was scheming to trick us.

"You can sleep on bunks in a cell, but you won't be locked in. And in the morning you can be on your way."

"Gee thanks," I said. "That's really great, but we want to keep going and get to New York." I couldn't see myself in a cell under any circumstances. Once we got there, someone else less friendly might be in charge.

After about twenty miles he dropped us off. Had he checked our IDs, he and I would have both been surprised. I found out later—much later—that Jim had been lying to me about his age and every-thing else. He was fifteen, a runaway from Sacramento, and his name was Glen. There was no such place as Wawee, Ontario. If we had gone to the jail there's a good chance some other cops would have found out Jim's age and held him there. Young Jim would have been toast, and maybe me too just for aiding and abetting a minor. If I had known he was only fifteen I wouldn't have let him travel with me. It wasn't cool to take advantage of my trusting nature.

One of our last rides as we crossed New Jersey the next morning was in a late-model Detroit sedan. As usual Jim got in back and I got into the front. The driver was a lady in her early thirties, casually elegant-looking with shoulder-length hair, and wearing a long coat. The windshield wipers were going because of a light mist and there was classical music on the radio. She adjusted the tuning when static interfered and asked me, "Do you like this composer?"

"I don't know much about classical music," I admitted, wishing I could say something less stupid about it to her. I liked her for asking about the music and I liked her even more for being unafraid to pick us up. In a world filled with menace and dread, women didn't stop to give guys a ride. Like myself, she was either unfazed by conventions or oblivious to them. She was the only woman driver to ever help me along in 22,000 miles. Before she dropped us off I gave her one of my *Paracutes* booklets.

Traces of the nineteenth and early twentieth centuries lurked just beneath the modern surface in New York. I tried to be blasé and not gape skyward. Down on the ground it was an atmosphere of old iron-work, weathered brick, Hebrew lettering, fruit stalls and wares in front of shops. Time here hadn't passed so much as accumulated in sedimentary layers. I was prepared to see horse-drawn wagons and carriages in the brick streets. The most modern touch that I noticed was REVOLUTION 66 spray-painted on walls everywhere.

Jim and I ambled through Washington Square Park, under the arch and past the fountain, with Darlene, Joe Knight, and a few other friends from Lincoln. Like me they'd aggregated here in the past weeks, all of us part of the latest wave of young invaders come to reconnoiter the aged city. By now I was over my angst about Darlene, and she was without the twerp who'd displaced me. We didn't resume where we'd left off, but we were back on friendly terms. She guided several of us by way of the Staten Island Ferry to her new lodging, a furnished room with a sloped ceiling at the top of a house. It was a nice place, much nicer than my dingy places in Lincoln had been.

"I'm not supposed to have visitors," she reminded us. "Just be real quiet."

We drank red wine and enjoyed the added benefit of New York, where you only needed to be eighteen to buy alcohol. It was a hot July afternoon and I sat in the easy chair and dozed with my shirt off. When I woke up I was confused to see writing all over me in lipstick and marker pen. Everyone had their laugh, including me, before I washed it off in the hallway bathroom.

With the increased intake of wine there got to be more distur-bance, enough that by evening the landlady came upstairs to investigate.

"Out! All of you," she said, and addressed Darlene. "You too. Out."

"Me? What do you mean?" Darlene said.

"Take your things. You're evicted."

"Aw, c'mon. It's our fault, not hers," someone told the woman.

"Don't kick her out," added another.

"We're going," I said. "Let her stay."

"Out, out, out. You have one hour to get all your things." She was adamant.

Darlene packed a suitcase and rounded up her few possessions in a plastic laundry basket and a couple of cardboard boxes. In a sobered and solemn brigade we helped get everything down to the curb. By now it was dark and I worried about abandoning her there. She surprised us by saying she had an aunt living on Staten Island. She called her aunt first, and then a cab to take herself and her stuff over there.

Meanwhile, a New Yorker in our group made a phone call to find a place for the rest of us, with no luck. Then another one located a friend in Queens, who offered us emergency shelter. Minus Darlene, we all rode the ferry back to Manhattan and then took the subway, which felt like another relic from the past, put there by ancient generations.

It was only sixty-some years old but it seemed much older. People who grew up riding the subway didn't realize what a novelty it was. How many cities in America had an underground railroad? More than anything else about the subway, I was disoriented by one of the lines on the map showing stops in Jamaica. Some geographic instinct took over and messed with my bearings. Despite all logic I wondered if the Caribbean island was nearer than I thought.

The furnished high-rise apartment in Kew Gardens was occupied by a middle-aged small-time scam artist and his younger partner in crime, two guys who had gained entry by fraud. Their racket was pretending to own vacant apartments they knew about and collecting cash deposits from prospective renters. I don't know how successful they were in getting money, overall.

The deal was that we could all stay for three days but then we had to go. Sounded fair enough. When Darlene joined us the next day, the scammers put her to work on the phone, reasoning that victims would be less suspicious of a woman's voice. She was half-hearted about it though. Sort of as a dare she talked to one person who responded about the intended apartment, while we all listened, but once off the phone she said she felt sorry for him. Cheating people wasn't our thing.

The dairy left deliveries at the door, and the scammers ordered large quantities of yogurt and orange juice that they had no intention of paying for. It was the first time I ever had yogurt, and the first time I ever saw groceries that listed, in addition to weight and ingredients, the mysterious message "Blessed by the Rabbi." I was hungry and ate the blessed yogurt with an untroubled heart. Cheating the dairy company out of a little cup of yogurt wasn't as heinous as cheating a person who was looking for an apartment out of a big wad of security-deposit money.

I was ready to turn Jim loose to fend for himself. On the road I appreciated having a wing man, but it felt like I'd been looking after him ever since we met. Greenwich Village had been his destination all along, not mine, so I launched him off on his lonesome, just as I had found him originally. I wouldn't have felt as guilty as I did if I'd known then that he hadn't been truthful with me in the first place. It wasn't my responsibility to look after a runaway kid. I heard that the police stopped him a couple of weeks after that, and when they found out he was fifteen, they shipped him back home to Sacramento. Strange that he was caught though. Unlike in Chicago, New York cops never once hassled me, or for that manner anybody that I knew.

By the fourth day we had an arrangement with someone else in the Kew Gardens building who said we could come in during the day, after his girlfriend left for work. She didn't want us there overnight, so we all slept on the gravel roof that night, Darlene and another girl included. The next morning I felt coated in the airborne grime that quickly attaches to you in New York, dirty and gritty, just like The Lovin' Spoonful's hit song that month. We waited for the all clear signal that the girlfriend had left and I was glad when we could go down to the apartment and shower.

In Greenwich Village Joe Knight and I roamed at night past the Cafe Wha? and other coffee houses that wanted a cover charge to walk in the door. We knew of it only from the belated word that had reached us on America's prairie via magazine articles and photographs. This bohemia went back to the turn of the century and even the beatniks and folksingers were late arrivals. Now we found an upscale tourist destination.

A girl we met persuaded a doorman to sneak us into the Cock and Bull without paying the cover, and we sat at a large table with her friends. We had to order drinks that were nowhere near as cheap as a beer at Adele's. We might have bought a coffee or a Coke, but one drink was all we could afford, and there was nothing going on there anyway, just a lot of crowds at tables, and the bright lights made me want to leave.

People like me weren't prosperous enough to gain admission to the counterculture folk scene. You know, the scene where entertainers like Peter, Paul and Mary sang plaintively about being five hundred miles from home.[1] To be exact, I was five hundred miles from Cleveland. Nobody wanted to hear my mournful song about being broke and hungry though, or to hear that I didn't even have a place I identified as home. They came to sit and look artsy and sip on overpriced drinks. That first impression of Greenwich Village always stayed with me: it was a place where you needed cash to be a down-and-out artist.

Being five hundred miles from home, Joe Knight and I settled down to sleep on some park benches in the warm July night. I took off my glasses and set them aside and in the morning they were gone. I looked around for them, then looked in the same places again, in disbelief, and then looked a third time before I was convinced they weren't going to reappear. It's always a surprise when things go missing, the way my box of poetry books had vanished in

Lincoln. Come to think of it, Joe wore glasses too, but he put them in his pocket that night and still had them when we woke up. Good thing I'd kept my shoes on. Someone with more common sense or more experience might have avoided the predicaments I managed to get myself into. Sleeping in kitchens, jails, corn fields, rooftops, and parks wasn't the carefree life on the road that I had originally imagined. Still, I preferred it over sleeping with a rifle under some rainforest bushes, and if all that I lost were my glasses, I could handle that.

Joe and I passed more REVOLUTION 66 graffiti on our way to Allen Ginsberg's apartment on East 10th somewhere down by Avenue C. It was considered part of the Lower East Side then, in the area later known as Alphabet City. I think we just found his address in the phone book. This time I wouldn't be tongue-tied before the Zen master. I was hoping to meet Allen in his own habitat and get to know some local poets the way I had in Cleveland. Peter Orlovsky answered the door.

"Hi Peter," I said. "Remember us? From Lincoln, Nebraska? We had a party at our place."

"I remember! Come in, come in. Sure, I remember Lincoln."

Some other people were there, packing up expensive-looking cameras and lighting equipment, and left shortly after we got there.

"They're making a movie about Julius," Peter said. A couple years later I did go to see the documentary film by Robert Frank, called *Me and My Brother*, about Julius, Peter, and Allen Ginsberg. Having met the three main characters, it was cool to see them walking and talking on a movie theater screen.

"Is Allen here?"

"No, he's away," Peter told us. Only he and his catatonic brother Julius were home.

Their apartment, what we saw of it, was no more lavish than any other East Side tenement I visited would turn out to be. Just as humble and unremarkable, it was. As we sat in their kitchen, Peter asked, "So you said you're from Lincoln? You saw us at the poetry reading?"

"We did! That was my apartment where we had the party with Karl Shapiro and Allen," I said. With a shy smile even Julius appeared to remember us. "Last month I saw Allen in Cleveland, too."

Now it was Peter's turn to be the host. "You guys hungry?" He opened the refrigerator. "How about some cold chicken?"

We were grateful for the snack and he took out some cold orange juice too. The bottle confirmed it was blessed by the Rabbi.

Then I told him how we'd slept in the park and my glasses were stolen.

"Junkies probably took them."

"What do they want with glasses?"

"That's how junkies are, man. They'll take anything, even if they can't get very much. They need money for drugs so bad that they'll break into your place from the fire escape to steal things." He was friendly with his advice about the perils and pitfalls of the big city. You had to be watchful in New York. I was still learning not to be so trusting of people.

We could have gone back another time when Allen was there but we didn't. I didn't ask Peter when Allen would return, either. I didn't want to show up again as a homeless beggar, which I remained for many months to come.

I didn't really need my glasses that badly. I first began wearing them in grade school when I couldn't read the blackboard from my desk, and now wearing glasses was mostly a habit. I wasn't helpless without them. In a phone booth in the Manhattan yellow pages I found a nearby address on Orchard Street, "Only One Flight Up" said the ad, where they made new glasses while you waited.

As Joe and I walked the mile or so, decorated with REVOLUTION 66, we came to an increasingly lower region of the Lower East Side, a habitat of Hasidic Jews in long sidelocks and black hats and coats.

Some of them must have been refugees from Nazi Germany or concentration camp survivors. Hebrew writing everywhere on windows and signs made me feel like I was in the Old Testament. Not only the green grocers, but every merchant had their wares out on the sidewalk in front of their store—racks of clothes and shoes, tables of dishes and bedding, lamps, furniture, books. It was a world away from Lincoln, Omaha, Chicago, or Cleveland. There was no sign of the orchard that gave the street its name.

We climbed a worn wooden stairway to a large and thriving business that was like a trip back to old Europe, just another antiquated facet of New York I was starting to grow used to. I was tested by a hunched older man who had a velvet-lined case with a collection of lenses arrayed in slots. He manually fit various ones into a holder for me to put on and read an eye chart with, until he determined which prescription was right for me. Instead of picking out heavy black frames like I had before, I tried on some other styles before selecting some octagonal ones of thin metal with fine filigree etching. Joe exclaimed, "They're you!" I wasn't sure what part of me they were: an ancient sage, a meek wimp, a stone freak?

The new glasses were made up while I waited, but I couldn't pay for them. I tried to emulate the scammers in Kew Gardens. "Send me the bill," I said. Did I really believe he'd copy down a phony address?

"We'll hold onto them for you," the man replied without a trace of mockery. "You can come back to pick them up when you have the money."

After a week or two I still didn't have a plan to get money for the glasses. Phoning my parents was out of the question. Remembering the generosity of the Simons, I telephoned Cleveland and explained my problem to Celeste. Her parents wired me twenty-five dollars and I picked up my glasses. I intended to repay them, like I'd repaid the girl in St. Louis for the bus ticket, but it would be a year before I had any money and by then I'd forgotten.

· · ·

Once again Joe Knight went his own way. I stayed at a crash pad in the East Village for several days and nights with a couple people I knew from Kew Gardens and a dozen or more others. We slept scattered around the wooden floor of an unfurnished three-room tenement apartment. Most people had somewhere to go during the day, some even leaving for work every morning, saving up enough money to rent their own place. Two older guys looked a little better off than most. "Older" to me meant late twenties or maybe around thirty. They wore nice leather blazers and polyester slacks and looked like they ate regular meals. Their beards and combed hair gave them sort of a Wolfman Jack appearance, slicker than most of us longhairs. One night they came in saying they'd been at a studio where Bob Dylan was doing some recording. They mentioned they were driving west soon and agreed to give me a ride. For all I knew they could have been ferrying a shipment of dope to Chicago, which would account for their prosperity.

On the morning that we rode through New Jersey the sky was gloomy and gray. Both sides of the toll road looked like a jungle of smokestacks, industrial towers and power grids. You wondered why this was called the Garden State. After an hour the driver had to pull over onto the shoulder so his friend could puke in the ditch, a performance which sort of went with the view that morning. The driver explained that the night before his buddy had some heroin that left him feeling queasy now. After that we had a smooth trip and they delivered me to Cleveland that night.

CHAPTER 11

I traveled lighter all the time, without the duffel bag any more. Soon all I carried was an olive drab army blanket, but no toothbrush or change of clothes or other niceties, and I was always glad when I could get a bath or a shower. I had a pocket comb and a thin wallet with a Nebraska driver's license and an expired student ID. I carried a notebook for poems and a journal of my travels, and a pen to write in it. The notebook was a green clothbound ledger with "Record" printed across the front, that I'd enhanced to read "Record of Mishaps." With little or no money, I usually didn't eat. Meals were no more predictable than the unlikely places I'd lain to sleep. The term "meal" was but a euphemism for a bite to eat, a sandwich, a hot dog, a pizza slice.

Back in Cleveland again, instead of at Diane and Phil's I stayed at another place in the same general area as Adele's Bar, I think Sue Weiss's. A familiar crowd was crashing on Sue's floor, including a friendly guy named Skip who I knew from Diane's. He was on the shorter side compared to me, in his early thirties, who said he worked in the Merchant Marines.

Skip and I were walking in the evening not more than a couple of blocks from Sue's, in an area near the university with lots of fraternity houses. We passed what looked like an open kitchen door. The light was on and it looked like there was nobody inside, so we edged up to have a better look, with the idea to snatch something from the refrigerator. Seeing that the coast was clear, we opened the screen door. Still no sign of anyone, so we tiptoed in. On the table stood two full grocery bags. We grinned at each other and Skip put a finger to his lips as a reminder. I began to sort through a bag, pulling a loaf of bread off the top. Skip whispered, "Take the whole thing," as he lifted the other bag. We scurried out with the groceries, down the steps, hustled along the sidewalk, and broke into a trot back to Sue's.

It was a windfall by any definition, enough to share with friends. I assumed it was a fraternity house, whose pampered kids were subsidized by money from home. They could shrug off the loss and I couldn't afford a regular meal, let alone college. Later I felt a bit of contrition, if not remorse. Not for the cost of the groceries, but for the bewilderment I caused some individual, frat rat or otherwise. Whether it was a private residence or a communal student home, I couldn't brush off the empathy I felt for the shopper who'd left the bags on the table. I pictured them coming back to the kitchen and being as confused as I'd been when my glasses were taken. I knew what that moment of disbelief was like, wondering how this could be. The sense of loss. I should have at least gone back and left them a poem in the mailbox. Instead I paid for my crime with karma.

A big party went down at Sue's place and the crowd included some of the bikers from Adele's. The next morning I couldn't find my Record of Mishaps. The apartment was mostly unfurnished, meaning there weren't many places to look for it besides behind the refrigerator or in the kitchen cabinets. I also checked the garbage cans outside. The Record had fifty or a hundred handwritten pages. It had the Polaroid of me and Dirty Ralph on Wells Street. I never took particular trouble to safeguard it, and wondered if it had been stolen.

I asked several people if they had seen it but no one admitted knowing anything. I suspected the bikers took it for a prank, not that

I was going to confront any of them about it. It was like my glasses. The loss. The disbelief.

It was the second time my work had gone missing, after the box of my books at the university. Had someone taken it for a souvenir? Should I be flattered? Had someone hated my writing enough to want to sabotage me? I sat down and rewrote one of my favorite poems from memory, before I forgot it. The first two verses went:

Deary my lady shall we soar to the sillybird fair
Where the carousel whirls in a thousandsoft starspinning
    candy reflections
And the ferris wheel whirls in the fluttersweet twinkling of
    night

Sparkle your eyes in the cascading brilliancy there
As we silence the sandman who whispers his dustydark
    sleepy objections
And dream while awake in the icecreamy flavors of light

A poem like this, that wasn't concrete poetry and didn't use profanities, that wasn't a complaint about the Establishment, that had meter and a rhyme scheme—a poem like this was guaranteed to remain obscure and unprinted in the mimeo revolution.

In both Cleveland and Chicago I knew a lot of street people and places where I could crash. In either city I'd get restless after a time and move on, before people grew tired of me. Funny that I was the only one who spent time in both cities though. I guess even most of the street people were close to their roots in one location or the other. I was the authentic wanderer.

There were more street people on Wells than on Euclid Avenue in Cleveland, and I seemed to know dozens of them, as aimless as me. We shared cigarettes and food and spare change. We kept each other company and passed the warm summer nights promenading and greeting one another. We began our stroll on the corner at North Avenue, at the wrought iron Old Town gateway spanning the sidewalk near the Stage Coach Restaurant. We passed Franksville and the lighted shops and clubs like Mother Blues, passed the bearded man dressed in red who sold popcorn from a sidewalk cart, passed the tourists and traffic. We turned and sauntered back again, with detours into Piper's Alley or Maiden Lane.

Jan worked in a women's clothing boutique on the less busy west side of the street, and spent her free time strolling with the rest of us on the east side, which is where I first got to know her. She was short and homely-looking, always cheerful and friendly, and seemed younger than most of us. Unlike the others, she usually dressed a bit classy, in skirts and new shoes, with her hair combed neatly in a short Mod style. I thought of her as Jan the Mod because I never knew her last name, like I didn't know most people's. She sometimes gave us spare change when we were panhandling for money to eat. By way of gratitude a group of us once nearly got her kicked out of her studio apartment when she invited us over and we started getting rowdy enough to disturb her neighbors. It was a lot like what happened at Darlene's place, except at Jan's there was no rule against visitors and we left when the neighbors complained, so she didn't get evicted.

Sometimes I fell in step with Mary, who I called Mary Mary, as in "Mary Mary, Quite Contrary." I didn't know her last name either. She was tall and wore a light shift in the July heat. She had an otherworldly smile and seemed to glide in a dreamy sleepwalk. As we drifted along we asked tourists for spare change, and when we had enough we'd buy a hot dog at Franksville. She reminded me of the kids in old Campbell's Soup advertisements, with wide-set eyes and a fresh-faced look. Even though her blondish hair was straight and chopped pretty short it would flop across her face, and instead of brushing at it she had a habit of puffing with her lower lip to blow it away. With only mild embarrassment she confessed that she had crabs and every once in a while would try to surreptitiously scratch herself, which on a crowded sidewalk we couldn't help finding comical.

In the quieter block of North Avenue around the corner from the Stage Coach Restaurant, I was alarmed to come upon Mary Mary one night, limping towards me. She had a squinched look on her face, sort of weeping in a half-concealed way.

"Mary? What's the matter?"

She shook her head.

"What's wrong?"

"I was raped," she whispered.

"What! When?"

"Just now. In the park."

She meant the park a few blocks over on Lake Shore Drive where I sometimes went during the day. She had walked from there and I was the first person she happened upon afterwards. She should not have been there alone in the dark of course. We all did stupid things, I wasn't the only one. Some things were more irreversible than others.

"Geez. Here, over here, sit down," I told her, and we took a seat on a dimly lighted doorstep.

"This man came up and held a knife on me."

"Just now you mean?" Even though I heard her the first time, the repetition might somehow make it more understandable.

She nodded. This was serious, but I didn't really know how to react. It was way over my head, too big to handle. I wanted to put a comforting hand on her shoulder but considered it might have an opposite effect. I told her I was sorry.

"Should I go look for a cop?"

"They won't do anything," said Mary and I knew she was right. Police were indifferent and there'd be no sympathetic assistance. I gave her a cigarette and went into the Stage Coach to get us coffee.

I tried to think of how else I could help and came up blank. There was nothing I could do except try to be a familiar friend. I asked if I could get someone and she shook her head. We sat drinking coffee and I made a lame remark that her attacker would get crabs. After a time she asked me to walk her to a house where she knew some people, and I took her there and left her at the door, hoping she'd be okay. I didn't see how she could put it behind her though. I was disturbed myself, perplexed by the vicious attack on my friend, and the brutality of people.

On a sunny morning while the shadows were still long and cool I ran into a girl and two guys I knew only slightly, a bit older and not hanging out on the street as often as some. However, we knew each other by name and they invited me to breakfast. I walked with them to a house a couple blocks past North Avenue where we had eggs and toast and coffee.

They asked if I knew anyone interested in buying crystal meth in large amounts. I didn't of course, because for one thing I didn't know anyone who could afford to buy more than a nickel bag of pot. I figured that these people had to be getting their large quantities from someone with even larger quantities, ad infinitum. There'd be a lot of money at stake and I wasn't experienced enough to know how to keep from getting either busted or ripped off. I also avoided getting mixed up with the meth and needle crowd, who if anybody ever fit the definition of drug abuse, the needle users were it. Speed freaks and junkies were both in the same class of ripoff artists who'd snatched my glasses that time I slept in the park. I had no desire to hang around those sorts, especially in any money transactions. It was more than I could manage, so I said I would ask around.

I had a liking for Billy Neighbor, another one of my street friends, a Chicago native. He seemed to have it together more than a lot of others. His real name was Nyborough or something that sounded like that and he called himself Neighbor. I talked to him about the three meth people, whose names he didn't recognize, and in a day or two I arranged an introduction out in the open on Wells Street. As I was meeting Billy I saw Lenny and Koos skulking across the street and down the block, shadowing us. They were two characters I knew by reputation and would not have trusted. I didn't even like their looks.

Koos was a tall redhead with a long neck in a faded olive drab army jacket, and Lenny was short and bulky in a navy pea coat. It was obvious Billy had gotten them involved but I didn't mention that I saw them. Lenny and Koos probably knew something about dealing, how to check the quality of the product, who to sell to, how not to be traced. I was just glad to take myself out of the middle and let them all negotiate without me.

For a second time I was yanked from Wells Street at night by the very same cop who'd arrested me before, Lieutenant Aguado. Seems like it was his turf. Without charging me with anything or patting me down he stuffed me into his car to await the paddy wagon that came and transported me to a jail cell again. The cells were furnished with metal benches welded to the wall, no bunks and blankets, and the lights were kept on all night. I was expecting the same treatment as the first time, but instead of going to a courtroom, I was released in the early dawn with no explanation. Didn't they know I was King of Valentine's Day? The cops at least could have given me a ride back to where they'd gotten me, instead of leaving me to find my own way back to Wells Street.

CHAPTER 12

S ome guy said, "Go west, young man." Something about manifest destiny. In August I decided to manifest myself west and stop in Lincoln again, with the idea to keep going from there to San Francisco. I didn't know what I was searching for. Something. I'd know it when I saw it, I guessed. Instead of trying to thumb rides I wrote my destinations on pieces of cardboard big enough to read from a passing truck or car. Trucks were my greatest hope because they usually were going some distance.

When I got to Lincoln it seemed like most everybody I knew was gone. I'd just been the first to evacuate. Some had left for the summer and some permanently, the way Darlene had gone to Staten Island. Frank McClanahan had moved into Steve Abbott's former apartment. Steve had moved with his aquariums of tropical fish to a one-bedroom apartment that was too small for any parties like he'd once had. Frank told me some of the old crowd was at a place Carl Davidson was renting to use as an SDS headquarters. I walked to a neglected old single-story house and found Grady and some of the guys hanging out. Davidson himself was away. He might have been visiting in Iowa, where later that month he was elected national vice-president of SDS.

"Hey Rhody. Where've you been?"

I told them about going to New York and seeing Darlene there, and Peter Orlovsky, and that I was on my way to San Francisco and needed a place to crash for a night or two.

"You can stay here with us."

"You sure it's okay? I never joined SDS."

"It's cool. You don't have to belong."

I was feeling inspired by the small-press publications of d. a. levy. I rounded up some materials for a smaller and more artistic project than my earlier fifty-poem tome. On yellow paper I mimeographed both sides lengthwise so that each half was identical, cut them in half lengthwise, folded the halves into thirds, and glued them into a construction paper cover. The front third was a title page with publication information, "4 suits by randy rhody, first edition 100 copies, copyright 1966, illusion press, lincoln, nebraskum." That left a small foldout with room for four short poems.

My friend George Eade let me have some glossy advertising posters that he'd salvaged from a printing plant where he worked. They promoted an insecticide, with magnified photos of flies and the words "Fight Back!" They were ideal for my fighting stance against the establishment. I cut them into small rectangles of partial graphics and glued them onto the covers with a border of construction paper still showing. The final result was as much a small work of art as it was a poetry chapbook.

I made one hundred booklets, gave a few away, sent a couple to d. a. levy, and mailed a few to the Peace Eye Bookstore in New York to put on their shelves. I took most of them with me on my travels to give copies to people who picked me up hitchhiking. The poems didn't have titles and the pages weren't numbered. Two poems per side could be read as verses of a single poem. All four could be verses, and it wasn't clear which side to read first. They were all four pretty unintelligible, to be truthful. Each line was sort of a free association with a picture I had in my mind's eye. No other reader would see that picture or have the slightest idea what I was writing about. There was no message or deep meaning. It was abstract writing, like abstract painting. It was art.[1]

When I went over to see Steve Abbott, I showed him my shoes that were worn through and falling apart. He offered me a pair of his own that he no longer had use for, black dress shoes that didn't fit me perfectly. At least the soles were in good condition and I could get my feet into them, so I put my old loafers in the trash.

While we talked he disclosed that he was gay. At a time when gays could be charged as felons, a confidence like that took some trust. Or instead of a confidence, maybe Steve knew that everyone except me had figured it out already.

"For real?" I said. "You?"

"Yes, it's true."

Almost a year I'd known him, and not suspected. I was oblivious, for sure, because it never occurred to me to wonder if anyone I met was gay—which by the way wasn't a term commonly used. Most people said fag.

What was I to say to his news? "Gee, sorry to hear it." Or at the other end of the spectrum, "Congratulations." To be honest, it wasn't a topic I was eager to find out more about. I was embarrassed, mostly. I couldn't manage to say more than something like, "Oh yeah? I didn't know that."

I assumed Steve meant he had gay inclinations. My innocent mind didn't reach far enough to wonder if he might have actually done some gay things with other gays, or if those activities could be the reason he now had his own apartment. I didn't take his admission as fishing to see if I harbored similar inclinations. Steve knew Darlene, and very well how unraveled I was when she dropped me.

At the SDS house some guys came in with a quiet, fiftyish black man, his beard beginning to go gray. His name was Edward English, and he'd just arrived in Lincoln on the Greyhound bus. He was looking for a place to stay and for help arranging a reading of his poetry at the university. He was equally urgent about contacting the Lincoln daily newspaper and having them print a story about him. From a duffel bag he produced a few newspaper clippings about his poetry readings in cities he had recently passed through, and a rumpled typewritten manuscript he titled *Nature's Creation*.

I was intrigued. Here was a man who seemed to have mastered the occupation of traveling poet, which I was only approximating. I wanted to talk to him about my own travels so far and the underground mimeo printing I had gotten involved in. I gave him a copy of *4 Suits* and asked whether he knew any small press publishers, or if he wanted help printing some of his poems here in Lincoln. While polite, he was also reserved. He wasn't as friendly as Clarence Major and I felt rebuffed. Other people, maybe Steve Abbott or Frank McClanahan, could be more helpful than me so I left him in their hands.

Next day a small article and photograph of Edward English was in the newspaper, naming the time and place of his reading in a small lecture hall on campus. At most a couple dozen people comprised the audience. It was summer, after all. His poems frequently reiterated the theme of "faith, hope, and charity"—all the things I was in short supply of. To me, he seemed from a mythic world of traveling storytellers and troubadors. He embodied a different kind of poet, sidestepping association with other writers. His method was idealistic and impractical. He was a solitary messenger without fanfare, seemingly the opposite of Allen Ginsberg.[2]

Although a self-described vagabond, he traveled by Greyhound bus from one place to another. He maintained a mystique about where he got money to travel, and why he had never been published, and what exactly he wanted to accomplish with the newspaper stories and readings. Those questions were never answered before he was on a bus to his next destination, with his latest newspaper clipping in hand. He was akin to the illiterate poet I'd written about in my high school poem, leaving no trace once he'd gone. But as with so many others from that year, I was soon to cross paths with Edward English again, entirely by coincidence.

Grady and two or three others were planning to hitchhike to Denver and when I said I was going that direction he suggested that we all go together. I recalled how difficult it had been for Joe Knight and me, just two of us, and I didn't see how a larger group would get many rides in uptight Nebraska. I thought it would be easier and faster to go separately by myself and meet them there. Grady named the Denver Folklore Center as a rendezvous point. He might have been there before, since his home town of Scottsbluff was on the western Nebraska border, only two hundred miles from Denver.

I started out for Denver a day or two ahead of the other guys, carrying my blanket and a small black valise that contained a loaf of bread and my poetry booklets. An early August wind blew the day's heat across the prairie and without a canteen I was soon thirsty. An occasional car blasted by and ignored my signal for a ride. Semi trucks left a backwash that fluttered my clothes and kicked up dust.

In the late afternoon when it seemed like I'd walked for hours a newer sedan pulled onto the shoulder. The driver was an older gent dressed in a suit and fedora hat. I got in the front passenger seat. The interior was immaculate. The car and proper suit were out of place on that barren land.

"You don't happen to have any water, do you?" I threw a hopeful glance towards the back seat as if by a miracle he carried a jug of ice water.

"No. Sorry, I don't."

"I've been walking a long time. I'm really thirsty."

"Would you like a lemon drop?" He held out a small cellophane bag and I took one. I didn't see how the little candy was going to hydrate me, but it helped my dry mouth, and after that we didn't have much else to say. He sat erect and untalkative. It was that Generation Gap thing.

After he dropped me off I walked some more miles and Steve

Abbott's tight dress shoes began to hurt my feet. A heel rubbed. The toes pinched on one side. I wished I had the holey-soled loafers I'd thrown away.

In the dark it didn't cool down much and I kept walking. A dim light appeared ahead and when I got near I saw it was a lone bulb over the front door of a white clapboard church or town hall. Not a soul around. Set back behind it farther off the road were a few scattered houses, their windows already darkened. I got a drink from a spigot in the wall and walked behind the building. In a back doorway where there wasn't any light I slumped down on a poured concrete step and took the shoes off and slept.

A couple hours later the luckiest thing happened. A car going by on the road slowed and then stopped. Grady and the others were waving out the windows and calling, "Hey wake up man, come on!"

"How'd you get here so fast?" I was never so glad to see friends.

"We got a ride straight through, all the way."

"Let me get my shoes and stuff." I began to sit up and then, more awake, I realized no car was around in front waiting for me to climb in. Shipwreck survivors must have such vivid dreams of rescue boats.

At first light I woke up from an agitated sleep, feeling lonelier than ever. There was no sign of anyone from the houses yet, so I drank from the spigot again and got moving. The plains were as indifferent to my well-being as they were to the bygone buffalo herds and native tribes. I may as well have been marching across an endless and windblown mid-continent in a previous age, when power lines and roads were not yet on the land. Those man-made things gave me no comfort now. The Heartland, it was called. It was plain that Nebraskans lacked heart. In the dozen other states I'd been through I hadn't had half as much trouble getting a ride.

America was indifferent too, except to put me in a uniform and ship my expendable carcass out. They'd have to hunt me down first. I was in a race for life or death. I wasn't sacrificing my tender years for someone else's Consumer Price Index. I had other plans, seeking some grail of highest perfect understanding, be it in Denver or elsewhere. I didn't know what that would be, something to do with Allen Ginsberg's "cloud" and the hand that didn't exist.

My feet were swollen and the shoes soon hurt even more. This was not how Edward English traveled. It was a desolate trek, miles of barbed wire with few meaningful rides. Starting ahead of the others had been a bad decision. Fence posts, wire, weeds, broken glass, rusted beer cans, a baking breeze that melted my energy. Short rides, long walks, short rides, long walks. A Bo Diddley song in my head kept me going, the one about walking forty-seven miles of barbed wire.[3]

About halfway to Denver I walked through North Platte. After the companionship of fence posts and telephone poles, the town seemed an oasis of civilization: gas stations with drinking fountains, motels, grocery stores, traffic. Still, none of it was a relief for me. I looked like a tramp. Cars were honking, people yelling at the longhair and after a while it started to bug me. When I heard the crunching sound of a car pulling up on the gravel shoulder behind me, I whirled around to defend myself, braced for more harangue and an unpleasant confrontation. Two smiling younger guys were waving at me. They had longish hair, definitely not establishment material.

"Hey, you need a ride?"

"Yeah," I answered. "I sure do." The door opened and the passenger tilted his seat forward so I could climb into the back.

"Wow thanks man," I said, glad to get off my aching feet and sit.

"We saw you hitchhiking and went to get my dad's car."

"That's great." I was just happy to meet some friendlies out in that forsaken place. "I haven't been getting many rides."

"Where you going?"

"Denver."

"We can take you a ways. Not very far I guess, just a ways. Where you coming from?"

"I was in Lincoln last, but I've been traveling around. Chicago and

Cleveland mostly. I met some poets there. I'm gonna meet some friends in Denver."

"Sounds cool."

"You guys live here, huh?"

"Yeah, we're in high school."

"I've been printing some poetry." I dug into my satchel and got two copies of *4 Suits* and passed them to the front. "Here, I put this together while I was in Lincoln."

The passenger took them and leafed through one. "Hey, that's really cool. We'll show this to our English teacher."

The driver glanced over at them and added, "Yeah, she'll like that. And we can tell our class how we met you."

We rode for about an hour and then they had to turn around.

"Wish we could take you farther. It's my dad's car," he repeated.

"That's okay, man. You helped me a lot. I'm sure glad you stopped."

"Good luck."

"Yeah. Thanks again. I mean it." I was sorry to see them go, not as much because of the ride as because of the loneliness that would soon return. Once again it was just me and the hostile wilderness.

Not long after, another late-model sedan stopped for me. The driver was an Ivy League type, wearing pressed slacks and a button-down shirt, too old to be a fraternity boy or draft age. The ash tray was full of quarters, dimes, and nickels. He was some kind of traveling church singer, played guitar and sang hymns, a real Jesus freak. He was going most of the way to Denver so I tried to be pleasant. Then he started in on some Bible talk and I knew it would be an ordeal. He'd made a record album of his church songs and when we stopped for gas he showed me a box of them in the trunk, and his guitar case. He didn't offer to strum a tune for me and I should have asked. If we didn't have any common ground in beliefs, we might have in music. He could have known some of the folk songs I knew, maybe knew about the Folklore Center. I could have saved him from religion.

. . .

When I got to Denver I found the Folklore Center but there were no messages from Grady on the bulletin board. I put up a scrap of paper saying I was in town and hung around out front. Two other guys occupied the sidewalk, a kid about sixteen with curly long hair on a skateboard, named Ergo, and a barefoot guy named John, sturdy-looking, with a sort of Dutch-boy haircut, blond, straight and chopped off just below his ears. He had a short beard and sometimes smoked a pipe. I asked if they knew where I could crash and they told me about this girl named Karen who had a closed-in front porch they were staying at.

The next day I checked the bulletin board again. Since there was no word from Grady I went up to Boulder to see Terry Tilford, the guy from Lincoln who'd taken me along to read my poems at Kearney State University. Steve Abbott had given me his address. Terry had left Nebraska and transferred to the University of Colorado, living in a campus dormitory. When I found him I presented him a copy of *4 Suits*. In the campus newspaper I saw that Edward English was there too, giving another one of his faith, hope, and charity appearances. I told Terry about seeing Edward English in Lincoln and we went to his poetry reading that evening.

I greeted him when we arrived, and of course he remembered seeing me only a few days before. When I remarked on the coincidence of our meeting again he seemed as impersonal as previously. His presentation was in an ordinary classroom with not much of an audience, a small group of us sitting at classroom desks. I wrote an acrostic poem with the first letters of each line spelling out EDWARD ENGLISH and passed it to him after the reading. He was talking to people who came up to him and as before I had the sense that he wasn't looking for any camaraderie so I didn't stay.

CHAPTER 13

When I got back to Denver, Ergo and John were still hanging around the Folklore Center, and Grady's group had arrived. He said they got a ride straight through all the way from Lincoln. During the trip he'd played his guitar and everybody sang folk songs. Maybe I was clairvoyant. It was just like the dream I'd had while crossing Nebraska, and lot more fun than the earnest Christian guitarist I rode with.

Karen, whose place we were staying at now, invited us all to a happening in Boulder but I was the only one interested in going along. For the occasion she wore some white painters shorts with suspenders, similar to lederhosen, that I thought looked weird but I didn't say anything. She was nearly as tall as me, very large-boned, with straight dark hair to her shoulders. In the parking lot outside the happening she produced a joint that we shared while we sat in her Volkswagen. We went separate ways inside.

There were a couple hundred people with a lot of alcohol, but no acid being handed out that I could tell, not like at the acid tests I had heard about. I got a paper cup and walked around asking people for a dollop of whatever they were drinking—beer, wine, or liquor of any kind. It was a light and music environment, only instead of a live band they played records. Shifting colors on the wall were from food coloring mixed with cooking oil that was wiggled by hand over transparency projectors. Intermittent strobe lights made me disoriented and each time I had to wait for them to stop. From one corner an elevated spotlight aimed at random people in the crowd who waved their arms or danced up and down or did some other small performance. When the spotlight landed on me I didn't have any tricks for the audience, so I froze and tried to ignore it until they got bored and pointed it at somebody more interesting. On the drive home Karen and I agreed the happening had been just okay, nothing to be excited about.

I walked into the Folklore Center and found Grady and others I knew sitting around. Hanging out with them was a bony, anorexic girl they introduced as Patty, pale and lightly freckled, with straight neck-length brown-blonde hair. She wore a dress and smoked a lot and shared her cigarettes all around. Accepting another cigarette, Grady said, "Patty's our benefactor." She could afford being generous with them because she worked part time as a waitress. When it came to haircuts, girls didn't have to change their looks as much as guys did to find jobs.

I gradually got to know Patty and went along when she stopped by her place, a spacious bare-bones two-bedroom basement apartment, one of many basements I found myself in that year. She stayed with two male roommates. A slightly pudgy guy a couple years older than us occupied one bedroom. He did childish acrylic paintings on cardboard-backed canvas panels, but he was no artist. He seemed to make his living accepting money from a thirtyish married woman who came by to spend afternoons in his room. The other bedroom was occupied by Joe, who was around forty and didn't look in great health. He sat in the kitchen a lot chain-smoking cigarettes. Patty slept in the front room, where a couple of twin beds against the walls served primarily as sofas.

All three of them were as chronically hungry as I was, and when Joe saw an ad in the paper for an all-you-can-eat spaghetti night at a restaurant, the four of us went together. We heaped our plates at the self-serve spaghetti table, and went back for seconds. After we got our third plate the manager came over to our table and told us we couldn't have any more. At least Joe and I would have gone for a fourth round. You'd expect All You Can Eat to mean, "Eat as much as you want." I guess he saw his profit turning into loss and read it literally as, "That's all you can eat. No more. Now leave." We should have demanded truth in advertising. We left peaceably.

Patty took me to visit a friend of hers whose husband was a policeman. I thought it was weird that several *Playboy* magazines were on the coffee table. He was away at work and Patty's friend gave her a key to his convertible, telling us we could take it for a drive the next night when he was sleeping. She asked only that we put gas in it when we were done so he wouldn't notice it had been driven. Maybe an offer to take his car was her payback for the *Playboys*. Sure enough, next night the convertible was parked at the curb and I got behind the wheel. It was a warm night and I put the top down and drove to a highway outside of Denver, sometimes pushing it up over a hundred miles an hour. The highway was deserted and we were flying. After a couple hours we put some gas in it and parked the car and walked back to Patty's.

She said if we walked down a certain alley on the way home, there was an apartment building where we could sneak into a swimming pool. We were quiet slipping into the water so no one would hear us, fully dressed except for our shoes. After about fifteen minutes we got out, dripping wet in the warm night, and continued along the alley. She said if we met any police to say we were coming from the dam. Seems like she had a natural instinct for criminal escapades and I was willing to be corrupted. At daybreak on another morning we traipsed across lawns stealing bottles of milk from doorsteps. We were a teenage Bonnie and Clyde.

Home from the swimming pool, we slept in our wet clothes in the living room, on top of the makeshift sofa, without drying off or getting undressed or getting under a blanket like sensible people. In a movie we would peel off our wet clothes and it would turn into a passionate night. In real life we woke up still damp. When Joe got up in the morning he must have formed the mistaken assumption that we had passed the night in the movie version, or else thought he would try to encourage us, because from then on he insisted we take his room, and he slept in the living room. Neither of us took the hint. Patty and I slept fully clothed each night on our own sides of his double bed. We just liked hanging out together, no pressure to be more than companions.

I walked down the street from the Folklore Center a few blocks to some shops that looked interesting. Inside a mod clothing store some weird stuff was playing over the sound system, people singing about brain police and freaking out in Kansas. The sales people were long-haired teenagers and showed me the cover of the double album *Freak Out!*. The Mothers of Invention were nothing like the British Invasion pop music and sentimental folk singers that still ruled radio. There weren't many customers and I loitered around and listened to the whole thing. A disembodied voice taunted Suzy Creamcheese. This wasn't Folklore Center material.[1] It was music for freaks like me.

So maybe happenings, joyriding, and Suzy Creamcheese weren't a total waste of my time. They were fun and everything but I didn't see the point in staying in Denver. We saw a notecard pinned to the bulletin board at the Folklore Center. A kid our age was driving to St Louis, 850 miles almost straight east. I guess he was going back to college and wanted to share gas and driving. In theory it was a four-teen-hour trip. The kid, Eddie, had a 1940-something Chrysler limousine built like a Panzer tank. It had rear suicide doors and a cavernous back area where we could really sprawl, with little fold-down jump seats that faced backwards. John, Ergo, me, and a couple other guys agreed to chip in for gas. I figured from St Louis I could easily hitchhike to Chicago. Patty was at work, so before leaving I wrote a letter, and I might have written a poem for her too. Joe said he'd be sure she got it. He looked a little disappointed that he hadn't successfully played Cupid.

I had confidence in the streetwise assurance of the other guys, but Eddie, even though he might have been older than some of us, struck me as kind of a mama's boy, in over his head with a car like that. He opened the trunk for our stuff, but among us we only had a couple of pathetic bundles to stow next to his luggage and boxes. We took turns sitting shotgun while Eddie drove and maybe later some of us alternated at the wheel. Whenever we stopped for gas or a break, Ergo would get out his skateboard and clatter around.

The monotonous hours passed and we pushed well into the Kansas night. Those of us in the back seat gradually dozed off. Suddenly I wakened and groggily noticed we were detouring across a newly plowed field. It seems the car had playfully sprung across the shoulder and cavorted over a ditch, and now it was bucking through the dirt and coming to a soft landing. We were all okay, but disgruntled, and Eddie sheepishly apologized for falling asleep. Ergo too, his co-pilot at the time who was supposed to help him stay awake.

That car must have weighed five thousand pounds and the massive tires were a few inches into the soft dirt. With the car in gear and everybody straining to push we still couldn't budge it.

"Push." Our feet slipped in the dirt.

"I *am* pushing." We grunted and strained.

"Hey Eddie, let me try." The tires spun.

"Put it in reverse." The car rocked about an inch and settled back.

Luckily, across the flat distance maybe a mile or so away we could see the lights of a gas station. John was the most sensible of any of us. He might've been older by a bit and was first to decide.

"I'm gonna walk over there and try to get a tow. You guys wait here."

During the long wait we sat in the car and went back to sleep. The station phoned for a tow truck from a nearby town and John waited to ride back with it so he could show the driver where we were. He told us that on his walk he'd seen a bunch of lights jumping around the sky, and the gas station attendant told him that a flurry of UFO sightings had been reported lately. John was a pretty straight-up guy, so I didn't think he was fooling with us with his story. (Cue The

Mothers of Invention singing "It Can't Happen Here.") We might have been abducted by aliens freaking out in Kansas while we waited for the tow truck, and then set back down in the field when they were through with us. Sort of a catch and release, like my history with the cops in Chicago.

The tow truck got us onto the road but something on the low-slung underbelly was broken and we had to be towed a few miles to a service garage in Junction City, Kansas, where again we slept in the car until they opened in the morning. Parts for that kind of car had to be ordered and the repair would take more than a day. We abandoned Eddie and his behemoth and I hitchhiked five hundred miles or so back to Denver with John and Ergo. I don't know why, since we were already closer to St. Louis and could've hitchhiked there just as well.

CHAPTER 14

I still didn't have money for a bus ticket and the lore among street people was that hitchhiking wasn't legal in Colorado, which is why I'd gone in Eddie's limousine in the first place instead of pushing on alone to San Francisco. A few days later I persuaded Tim we should try our luck with a freight train. Tim was from Chicago, where I first met him on Wells Street, as tall, gangly, and long-haired as me, but more fine-featured and very pale. Like many of us who wandered in those days he'd made his way to Denver just to see some place different.

Neither Tim nor I knew a thing about riding trains, but how hard could it be? I figured it would be a way to vault ahead in great leaps. I hadn't read *On the Road* yet, about stuff Jack Kerouac did twenty years before us. I was under the impression that it was about riding freight trains. When I did finally read it I found out he rode buses in that book, not freight trains. And he was ten years older than me when he did it. Oh yeah, and when he needed money he phoned home.

Karen was the only person we knew with a car, and after she got off work she took us to the rail yard. In the last light of sunset we climbed out of her Volkswagen and said goodbye, asked her to wish us luck. Right away we met a worker in an engineer's cap and bib overalls.

"Is there a train going toward San Francisco?"

"Not tonight. This here one's going to Lincoln, Nebraska. She's pulling out in a few minutes." Lincoln was familiar ground at least.

"What do you say, Tim? Should we head east?" Right now any place was preferable to Denver. I'd try for San Francisco some other time.

"Sure. We can get to Chicago from there."

We'd imagined we would be getting into the cozy shelter of a boxcar like they do in the movies but the man said there wasn't time to look for one. With mere minutes to choose we climbed onto the first spot he showed us, a steel ledge projecting from the front of a hopper car. It was the kind of open-top container like a coal car, a gondola that angles inward at both ends. Between our small platform and the sloping front of the steel cargo box above us a sort of lean-to was formed. Steel uprights at each corner of the ledge connected to the lip of the car, strong enough to hold onto if we wanted to stand, but it was more comfortable and safer to sit. Our perch was just big enough to catch an overnight ride five hundred miles from Denver to Lincoln, maybe nine or ten hours, rolling along somewhere in a string of a hundred or a hundred and twenty cars.

When we started moving and adjusted to our night vision we contemplated the big lethal metal wheels of the car in front of us.

"Man, those'll slice you in half before you know it."

"I wouldn't wanna get my foot caught in that coupling down there either."

I flashed on our mangled bodies catapulted in a derailment, and blanked it out of my mind right away. It wouldn't do any good getting in a panic over imaginary disasters, since nobody was gonna stop to let us off any time soon. There was nothing we could do at this point except hang on. From where we sat it was a rumbling roaring steel juggernaut and at first it was kind of fun, a novelty. As we crossed the prairie we passed small towns and road crossings, sometimes not equipped with warning lights, where cars waited. Their headlights caught us for a moment as we sped by.

"Hey Tim," I said, "I wonder if they saw us."

We both laughed. "Yeah man, I bet they were surprised!"

At the next few lonely crossings we passed in the dark we waved towards any headlights, but then we got tired of that, going by so fast nobody had time to honk at us anyway, or else the train noise kept us from hearing them.

There was no stopping this shaking avalanche of metal that we'd jumped onto. Even in August, the hours after midnight had us shivering in the wind chill and kind of wishing we could get off. We huddled back-to-back, sharing a thin army blanket and trying to get warm, not saying much. We would have frozen to death before either one of us dropped our pride and put our arm around the other to conserve body heat. This was no tame amusement park ride that passed for a lark among boys our age in the Coney Islands of America. We were going to ride the dragon for hours to come, on the night wind across the Great Plains under the starlight. Some day we might remember it as an adventure, but that night was as much fun as tumbling down a canyon in a flash flood.

We'd never met anyone who in fact had ridden a freight train. In the backs of our minds we might have accumulated songs and stories and other cultural implants we weren't even aware of that inspired us to try this escapade. It was an American tradition we thought we could perpetuate. Jack London wrote a fabulous book in 1907 called *The Road*, his true account of traveling the railways with tramps, dodging the railroad cops and scrounging up meals. Compared to him, Jack Kerouac on the road was kid stuff. During the Thirties the freight trains were crowded with hoboes and ordinary men looking to get somewhere and find work. And when I was a kid there was a song on the radio that went:

> *Freight train, freight train, going so fast.*
> *Freight train, freight train, going so fast.*
> *I don't care what train I'm on,*
> *as long as it keeps rolling on.* [1]

In the morning we rode through monotonous fields for what

seemed a couple hours. The train halted in an endless expanse of corn with no sign of a town and we weren't sure what to do next. Along the gravel track bed a railroad worker came walking our direction. I was worried he would kick us off, but since we couldn't hide, I asked how long we would be stopped. He said it would be a while so we jumped down to stretch and warm up in the sun.

A white two-story farm house stood fifty yards away in the midst of the fields. Tim and I walked over to tap on the back door and then stepped back down to the ground. Every farm house I've ever been to had a front door for looks, but the back door was what everybody used. A plain sort of woman opened the door and regarded us through the screen. She had the uncitified look of someone who spent more time feeding chickens than idly polishing her nails.

The first thing she said was, "You want some water?"

"Yes please."

After a moment she brought two jelly-jar glasses and nudged the screen door open to reach them out to us. I drained my water, well water no doubt, which was warm from the pipes and even kind of dusty tasting.

"Thank you, ma'am," I said.

"Thank you, ma'am," Tim repeated.

"You're welcome." She wasn't especially genial. I gave her a lot of credit though, because she was kinder than all those Nebraska drivers who had passed me on my way to Denver. The farmhouse murders that Truman Capote wrote about had been not so very far away. People out in those wide lonely spaces, used to a trusting way of life, had reasons to be wary of strangers.

"I guess you knew we were thirsty when you saw us, huh?"

"A lot of people riding the trains come by."

"Oh." We handed our empty glasses back. "Well, thanks again."

We got back on the gondola platform and before long the train jolted and started rolling. When our train stopped in Lincoln, Tim and I were all too glad to jump off. We walked into town and over to the SDS house where I'd stayed a few weeks earlier going the other direction.

. . .

In a day or two we talked each other into going back to the rail yards to continue on to Chicago. This time it was afternoon when we got down by the tracks and we thought we could look around at our leisure and then depart in the warm daytime. Maybe it made sense just to get on any train and see where it took you. We didn't see any yard workers and climbed into an empty red boxcar without knowing if or when it was leaving. We soon discovered it was being coupled with some other cars. A locomotive slammed back on the line and the force cascaded along to our car and threw us off our feet, sending us skidding to the far wall. We jumped down and went to sit in some tall grass to contemplate our next move.

"Hey look at those guys," said Tim. On a train that was just rolling out of the yard I saw two older hobo-types standing in the doorway of a boxcar.

"They look like they know what they're doing."

"I wonder where they're going," he said.

"I wonder if they care where they're going," I said. Beyond Chicago, I didn't have the slightest idea where I was going. I could no longer claim kinship to the safe and secure college population. I saw myself transformed to a humble peer of those guys in the boxcar.

The afternoon passed before we approached a worker, an older man in work gloves who showed us a train that was leaving for Chicago in an hour or two.

"Can we ride in a boxcar?" I wanted to be sheltered out of the wind and enjoy the view from the open door of a boxcar, like those guys we'd seen earlier.

"All the boxcars are locked shut on this one." He showed us some flatcars with truck trailers lashed to them. "Right there between the rear tires is the best place. Under the axle."

"Really? You mean it?" It didn't look any better than a gondola car.

"Yep, that's where fellas ride. It's the safest spot. Those things are tied down good and you're protected by those big tires." We looked at the double wheels on each side, wheels that weighed more than we did.

"We'd be smashed if it fell on us."

"Shucks, those axles are strong. It'll never fall." He was right of course. How many trucks going down the highway suddenly had the back ends drop out from under them?

"Now you boys wait here, and I'll be back later and tell you when you need to get on."

It was about an hour before sunset when he returned and told us to get ready. We got up on the flatcar where we could sit leaning against the tires or stretch out, but we wouldn't be able to stand. There was nothing to hold onto except the truck axle if need be. He waited with us until it started rolling and gave a friendly wave. "Good luck, boys."

Again we rumbled and roared and shivered through the night, five hundred and fifty miles across Iowa and Illinois. Early next morning when the sun was up the train stopped. A man working with the trains came along and I asked, "Is this still going to Chicago?"

"Yeah, we just need to switch a few cars. We'll be going again in about twenty minutes."

"Where are we?"

"Iowa. You want some coffee?"

"Sure." He took us to the hospitality of a workman's shack where they gave us some coffee and let us use the toilet. This was the fourth time that nobody seemed to mind us being around the trains. It wasn't like the railway bulls you heard about that chased people and beat them with clubs in Jack London's day. Maybe the men were amused at two boys like us and took an interest in helping us be safe. They got us back on the train before it was due to pull out. Still there were no open boxcars, but the sun was out and we would be spared the cold for the rest of our trip, back under a truck trailer on a flatcar.

We were pretty uninterested in the view of fields and small towns as we crossed Illinois, just patient and certain we would get where we wanted to go in two or three hours. All in all, it was more direct than trying to hitchhike, which is how I usually got around the country, but I never rode another freight, and never did get to ride in a boxcar.

Tim still had his own room at his parents' apartment, and stayed there when he wanted. It didn't quite register with me that most of the street people I knew in Chicago had a backup shelter because they came from there or a nearby suburb, unlike myself, a homeless gypsy. Tim brought me home and we ate sandwiches, showered, and I washed and dried my clothes. I said so long and took the 'L' to Old Town.

CHAPTER 15

I asked around and ended up sleeping on the wood floor of a crash pad on North Avenue between Wells and Sedgwick, along with several other people, a mixture of runaways, teenyboppers, high school dropouts, and homeless. There was always someone who knew of a place where a person could crash, on condition that they or somebody else there could vouch that you weren't a needle freak or ripoff artist. After everyone recognized you, whoever answered the door would let you in, and likewise I would answer the door and let people in if I knew them.

I wasn't sure who paid the actual rent for some of those apartments. I guess a few people had money and allowances, like this girl who was wearing a sheepskin jacket I admired. She said she could buy me one with her mom's credit card. I didn't take her up on it. I hardly knew her and couldn't figure out why she'd want to buy me something so expensive.

For the next few nights I promenaded up and down Wells Street with Dirty Ralph, Pepper, Jan the Mod, Friendly Fred, and a slew of others on the street. I was still wearing Steve Abbott's ill-fitting black dress shoes, the ones I had worn to Denver. One of the street people on Wells claimed he didn't like the new suede cowboy boots that he was wearing. They were beautiful tan Fryes with round toes and western heels, pricey enough that his parents probably paid for them. He liked my shoes. Right there on the sidewalk we exchanged boots and shoes to try on for size, and agreed to a permanent trade. I thought he was bonkers, but kept my mouth shut.

It was mid-September and I turned nineteen. Jan the little Mod girl appeared with a giant department store paper bag and said it was my birthday present. It contained a new pair of corduroys, two sweaters, and a long winter scarf. I might have declined a hypothetical gift like the sheepskin jacket, but these were physically at hand. I was pretty speechless. My humble "Thank You" didn't quite seem adequate. I tried them on and everything fit me. With my new boots and these new clothes I was outfitted for cold weather ahead. If I had the sheepskin jacket I'd be one Marlboro cowboy.

Jan said she had shoplifted the clothes. I found it pretty hard to believe, given the shopping bag, but I didn't press her further. I guess she wanted to sound streetwise, but she just wasn't the criminal type, and how was it possible to shoplift so much stuff? The Sedgwick kids couldn't even shoplift salt and pepper. She might have used her own money, or had parents who gave her a credit card. It seemed like many of the street people weren't as desperate as me.

In all my life, I hadn't encountered too many examples of outright kindness. Her generosity and thoughtfulness puzzled me. We were friendly and everything, just like all the other Wells Street loiterers, but not especially close. She didn't act like she had an interest in me, and had even tried to set me up with another girl one time.

It was no surprise when I was pulled off the sidewalk again by my old nemesis Lieutenant Aguado for the crime of having long hair, for a third time hauled off in a paddy wagon to overnight accommodations in a cell. I was starting to feel like a repeat offender. I would have felt bad about being arrested but I hadn't done anything to feel guilty about. Based on previous experience, I relaxed and waited for morning. Bored, I broke off some chips of paint that was peeling to keep in my wallet for a souvenir. Once again I was released without even going to the courthouse. No charges and no explanation. The next evening I was back on Wells Street.

Big Brother and the Holding Company were playing at Mother Blues. They were from San Francisco and that was enough recommendation for me. We were just beginning to hear about the San Francisco bands by reputation. Only Jefferson Airplane had an album out, the one with the postage-stamp cover design, before Grace Slick replaced Signe Anderson. Big Brother didn't have a record album or songs on the radio and I knew of them by name only. We all wanted to see them, but you had to be twenty-one to get in. One of the kids on the street was Billy Blue and even though his mom owned the club he couldn't get us in.

At the place where I was crashing on North Avenue we were put on notice that one of the band members would be staying there for a few nights. Although most of us slept on the hard floors anyway, one of the bedrooms that had a mattress on the floor was declared off limits, reserved for the musician.[1] I didn't see any new faces and maybe he ended up not staying there, but in exchange we got a table at one of the September shows, despite our ages. I wasn't sure why I was invited, since it wasn't my apartment. Even though I developed an aversion to Chicago because of the cops, I got a lot of breaks from people I met in that town.

Mother Blues was a pretty small club and six or eight of us huddled around a table off to the side and ordered Cokes instead of beer or real drinks. I didn't recognize any of the songs, and we didn't know the musicians by name. Big Brother and the Holding Company didn't look like entertainers in stage costumes or matching suits like the Beatles. They weren't dressed much different than we were. The guys had hair down to their shoulders that signaled San Francisco origins. The female singer with the raspy voice also had wild long hair and looked more like a street person than a polished Dusty Springfield or Marianne Faithfull. Jefferson Airplane was the only other group fronted by a female. During the performance she introduced the band members and herself. Janice, it sounded like. During the break she walked over to acknowledge our table of longhairs with a brief hello. Nobody'd heard of her, and the billing for the show didn't mention Janis Joplin.

Since I'd made it only as far as Denver on my first try, going to see Big Brother reminded me of my ambition to set foot in San Francisco. First I wanted to check in on d. a. levy and other poetry doings in Cleveland. That week I persuaded my new friend Gallagher to hitchhike there with me. He was on the shorter side, with a cockiness to make up for it, blonde, wavy hair just over his ears, someone I got to know on Wells Street. We'd got into some giggling fits smoking joints together and other mischief, and got to be pals. Our progress to Cleveland was slow. We passed the polluting industrial stacks of Gary, Indiana. A car slowed for us and pulled onto the shoulder. Elated, we hurried to catch up and as we got near the car took off. Another wise guy taunting us, we figured.

By late afternoon we'd come about a hundred miles, trudging through Mishawaka, Indiana. The sound had a great rhythm to it.

"Mishawaka," he said.

"Mishawaka," I answered.

"Indiana," he said.

"Mishawaka, Indiana," I said.

"Mishawaka, Indiana is where it's at," he said.

"Mishawaka, Indiana is where it's at," we chanted together. We got a couple more rides by the time it was dark. At last a box truck stopped. The sleepy middle-aged, slightly Italian or Mexican driver with a black mustache was going to Cleveland and wanted someone to talk and keep him awake. Gallagher assigned me to the task and soon dozed off on the passenger side, so I had to keep thinking up things to say. I didn't know anything about sports or politics, two sure-fire ways to get someone wound up. I was never any conversationalist to begin with and what could I say to a guy old enough to be my dad?

"How long you been driving?" I asked him.

"Oh, about twelve years."

"No, I mean today."

"Oh. Yeah. I started out at six o'clock this morning." He yawned.

"Where from?"

"I started out in Akron. Had to make a delivery over by Chicago and now I'm goin' back."

"Almost there, huh?" He took his eyes off the road for a moment to glance at me and nod, his eyelids half shut.

"By the way, what time is it?"

"Huh?" I could swear he was sleeping with his eyes open.

"I asked what time is it now?"

"Oh. Yeah." He trailed away dreamily and I gave up and studied the road. Every time he swerved out of his lane I reminded him to wake up. He dropped us off in Cleveland late at night and I was relieved to be at our destination in one piece.

Levy was still up when I knocked at his door. A cautious voice from the other side asked, "Who is it?" and I answered, "Ambrose Bierce." Gallagher had no idea who Ambrose Bierce was, but I figured d. a. levy would recognize the literary allusion.[2] Levy opened up to let us in and welcome back the disappeared.

We sat in his kitchen and I told him of my ramblings since my last visit. Levy went in the other room for a moment and came back with a copy of the Cleveland *Plain Dealer* that he had been saving. He showed me a full-page story about the open-mic poetry reading we'd gone to some weeks earlier at The Gate. My picture was one of three, showing me at the podium reading to the audience next to the candle stuck in a wine bottle. Below the black-and-white photo was my name, spelled correctly for a change. The headline read, "lost? u r not alone" in mimicry of the style some poets were adapting. The reference to being lost was from the line in my poem. A portion of the article included a description of the stage presence I'd assembled to look the part. "A poet named Randy Rhody walks to the front of the room. He is wearing a red woolen sweater and a gold muffler. He is tall, thin and has long, well-combed hair. He reads..." It was followed word-for-word by the poem I let the lady reporter copy that night in July:

> *throw your suitcases out in the rain*
> *then hurry like nonsense and vanish*
> *into the night...*

Between my picture, the poem, and the description of me, I took up one-fourth of the entire page. I was elated and also sort of embarrassed. My poem wasn't that wonderful, but at least it wasn't political or obscene, which is probably why they printed it. Another photo showed Levy with a group of poets I'd met that night and other times, including Kent Taylor, rjs, and D. R. Wagner. The one other poem quoted was a semi-humorous depiction of humans as perpendicular porpoises, credited only to "anon." I liked it better than mine. The newspaper was days or weeks old, and there weren't copiers then, or if there were, not commonly available to make a copy to keep for myself.

Gallagher was a down-to-earth sort, not interested in poetry or literature. His main interest was in getting stoned, but he was impressed to see me in the newspaper. When I had first told him that Levy was a well-known poet-publisher, I didn't realize myself how influential he was. I overlooked that aspect and thought of him as a friend like Steve Abbott, the sort whose door I could knock on late at night. For the next few weeks wherever we went Gallagher was still telling people how he'd met the poet d. a. levy.[3]

I didn't look up the Simons to show them my new glasses and thank them for the money they had sent to me in New York. I was too embarrassed to face them and admit I had no way to repay them. They likely had seen the same newspaper story about the poetry reading at The Gate and I rationalized that sending me the money had been their usual way of supporting the arts.

It was the last time I visited Cleveland. I'd been there so many times that I assumed I'd be back again. When I left any place like Cleveland or Chicago or Lincoln, I didn't say *adios* to anyone in particular. I'd get the impulse, the wanderlust, and just up and leave, vanishing into the night without a suitcase, like my poem said. It didn't occur to me to suppose anyone missed me or wondered where I went. It was the same with arrivals. I'd kind of reappear and might or might not explain I'd been to New York, Cleveland, Chicago, Lincoln, or Denver.

After a few days Gallagher and I continued on to New York. I located Darlene there and led her and Gallagher in search of the fabled Peace Eye Bookstore. An Eye of Horus hieroglyph with falcon markings was painted on the store front, the same symbol d. a. levy had used in some of his printings. It didn't have anything to do with peace, but it looked cool and arcane amid the Hebrew lettering of Lower East Side shops.

Inside I found the copies of *4 Suits* that I had mailed from Lincoln two months earlier on my way west to Denver. I was so honored to see them displayed on a lower shelf that I didn't mind so much that none had sold. By now I didn't have many copies of my own left. The book store had some of Levy's stuff as well and I wanted to speak to someone at the counter but shied away. Guys like Matt Shulman and d. a. levy might be mortal, but to me Ginsberg and the Peace Eye were legends. Hesitating like I did, I hadn't figured out yet that all those people knew each other, and if I was a friend of one I'd be a friend of all. Two of the Fugs, Ed Sanders and Tuli Kupferberg had started the Peace Eye. I felt insignificant next to the eminent stature I imagined these poor writers held. If I'd had a copy of that *Plain Dealer* story to show them, or foreseen that in a couple of years I'd be published in the same anthology as Levy, Ginsberg, Sanders, and Kupferberg, it might have given me confidence. It was a missed opportunity to meet the New York poets and ricochet away on a new trajectory.

. . .

After we got back to Chicago I didn't mention the newspaper story to anyone on Wells Street. I kind of forgot about it. Chicago was a different crowd and it was another day. On the street I was a nobody without a past, coming from no place, going nowhere. Lieutenant Aguado hustled me into a squad car for the fourth time that summer. I should have had the newspaper with me to show him I was a renowned figure in literary circles. Passed him a copy of *4 Suits*. He would have been impressed.

He left me in his car for a long time while he went in search of another victim. In all the times he had arrested me he had never patted me down or had his lights flashing. I considered jumping out and running, but guessed if he caught me he could make a more serious charge than the usual lame accusation of loitering. Even if he didn't catch me, he'd be back looking for me another night and no telling what he would do. All the same, even though I supposed this would be the usual overnight routine, as I sat in the back seat I had the sick sinking feeling I got whenever he arrested me.

I sat there for so long that some of the regulars on the street saw me and I heard them calling to others how "the cops got Randy." People started passing the word, and then Jan and Gallagher and a few others came over and saw me for themselves, sitting there with a glum look like I'd been rounded up by the dogcatcher. The paddy wagon arrived to take me in and I was put in a cell, resigned to a long unpleasant night. To my surprise it wasn't long before a jailer appeared and brought me out again.

Jan and Gallagher were at the counter, having come to bail me out. It astonished me that anyone would go to the trouble to rescue me. My own family wouldn't have bothered. Jan said they took up a collection to get the twenty-five dollars needed to get me out. I was so grateful to be out of that cell, I really believed that several people had pitched in. I vowed to myself that I would go to court and get their money back for them. Quite possibly it was all Jan's money, like with the new clothes. I hardly knew her, and knew nothing about her. Was she a guardian angel assigned to my desperate case?[4]

CHAPTER 16

I had that Chuck Berry song in my heart, the one about Route 66.[1]
I wasn't looking for kicks though. After a couple weeks in
Chicago I was itching to be on the move again.

"Hey Gallagher, let's go out to Frisco." Our trip to Cleveland and
New York had proven Gallagher was roadworthy.

"In a day or two, man. I gotta do some stuff first."

"Not through Denver though," I said. "That time I hitchhiked
through Nebraska was a drag. We'll go down Route 66 through Los
Angeles and then head north."

"Sure, why not?"

Then two girls we sorta knew from the street clamored to come
along. The concept of four hitchhikers together was unreal. I figured
it needed to be tested and proven. I wanted to push the hitchhiking
limits, so I said okay, but they couldn't bring a lot of stuff.

Don't get me wrong—Jude and Tink were not at all our two
mates. Oh no. If they made a movie about us, the girls would be
gorgeous models in granny dresses and headbands, and we would be
brawny hunks in bead necklaces and sandals, with faces like men in
ads for cologne. In the movie we'd smoke a lot of dope and there'd be
an undercurrent of intrigue among us.

Except the Sixties weren't like the movies. Tinker Bell was a scrawny elf in worn corduroy and Jude was baby-fat chubby in a red and black hunting-plaid wool jacket. As for Gallagher, he was kind of a leprechaun. When we got high I thought he looked like a blonde Howdy Doody in a jean jacket. Me, I was a beanpole scarecrow in cowboy boots, with lanky hair hanging to my chin. Nobody would be impressed with us, or want something from us. They'd have to fabricate some drama for the makings of a movie because we didn't care about anything. We were too broke to have any dope and nothing was at stake, except our freedom.

Outside Chicago in the early October afternoon we got our first ride pretty quick from a straight type around thirty, driving a Detroit four-door and giving off family-man vibrations.

"Where you heading?" he asked.

"LA," we said.

"You from Chicago?"

"Yeah, we just started this afternoon."

"Me too." Seemed like he was willing to take us along for quite a distance. He didn't say he could take us for a hundred miles, or to the next city, or for two hours. It was open-ended.

The AM car radio played songs we liked, embellished with intermittent crackling and buzzing. Between Chicago and St. Louis there were plenty of good stations blanketing the state. Every time the Four Tops came on with "Reach Out I'll Be There" and sang "Just look over your shoulder," the girls would join in and comically whip their heads around to look over their shoulders.

I didn't ask people about their business, not being nosy or much for conversation. I was content to look out the window unless the driver wanted to make small talk. It was the girls who started it, with their chatter. He was doing the *Rabbit, Run* thing.

"You're leaving your wife?" Tink threw the one-punch.

"And baby?" Jude supplied the two-punch.

"We don't get along any more." Life was too much and he'd acted on a wild impulse to escape. Still, he had a framed portrait of her in a box of stuff in the back window.

"Ooh," went Tink. "She looks nice."

"That's so sad," moaned Jude.

They keened in unison. He gradually became more taciturn and I wished they would shut up and leave the guy alone. I saw they were putting a guilt trip on him that wasn't going to endear us if they kept it up.

He wanted distraction, not reminders. After dark, in the intermittent lights along the highway, he noticed a solitary woman in a red car in the next lane. They started waving to each other and soon began leap-frogging with their cars, first one pulling ahead, and then the other, and after a time both cars pulled off at a brightly lit service station. They touched noses and wagged their tails while the attendant gassed their cars and we used the rest rooms.

When we took to the road again he told us, "She's going to lead the way to a motel up ahead. I'll have to drop you off when we get there." She was turning out to be a better diversion than the four of us.

"Ohhh. That's not a good idea," Jude whined.

"You should go back to your wife," Tink whimpered. In my mind I agreed with them, and at the same time I had a twisted sort of admiration and curiosity. It was pretty amazing that just out of nowhere he picked up this blonde. Geez, on the highway at that. I concluded I was missing some kind of major ability of human nature. In all my vast and worldly nineteen years nothing like that had ever happened to me.

We'd made it halfway through Illinois, a respectable ride, although he'd've taken us further if the girls had kept their mouths shut and that woman hadn't appeared. He'd been decent enough not to leave us at the gas station. Later that night in another car we crossed the Mississippi past the new gateway arch in St. Louis, 300 miles out of Chicago.

. . .

The next morning in Missouri we stood clustered as a group. Watching all the cars pass us, I saw that the four of us were too intimidating so I had a bright idea.

"Listen. Cars'll stop for you girls. You two hitchhike and Gallagher and me will stay off to the side. If someone stops, explain there's four of us and ask them nice if they'll take us all."

A few times people offered to take just two of us, but we stuck together. Surprisingly, enough people were willing to load up four young passengers. We rode through a gray drizzle, passing wagon trains and looking across the fields at settlers' cabins.

Jude remarked, "Oh look, some mules."

"Missouri mules," said Tink, with interest. As if mules were a definitive landmark of Missouri, the way the Statue of Liberty was in New York. They could have been right, because I never saw mules anywhere else.

It was overcast but no longer raining and the four of us stood outside of Joplin. A sheriff's car pulled over to check us out and we each produced some ID. We were all either eighteen or nineteen, meaning we were old enough not to be hauled in as juvenile runaways. The deputy was a pretty friendly older man in a Smokey Bear hat.

"Are you in the Peace Corps?" In his mind I guess we looked less like dropouts and drifters and more like eager young idealists.

"No sir."

"Where you kids going?" he asked. People always seemed to think we were just going a few miles.

"Los Angeles," said Tink.

He didn't bother us about hitchhiking or warn us to stay off the road. After a bit he wished us luck and went on his way. By the second night we'd made it 700 miles out of Chicago to eastern Oklahoma.

. . .

It was a cool night and while walking we kept our eyes on the pavement just ahead. "Watch out for rattlesnakes," Tink cautioned. "They like to crawl out and lay on the warm road."

"Don't say that, man," I said. It freaked me out. The highway promised to be a mine field of deadly snakes waiting in ambush. Mules in Missouri, rattlesnakes in Oklahoma.

There weren't many cars and I was glad when a couple square types in button-down collars stopped for us. The passenger got out to let three of us into the back seat of the two-door, and Gallagher said he'd sit in front between the two men.

"Uh uh. Guys in back. One of the girls sits in front," the passenger demanded. Tink said she'd do it and the rest of us squeezed into the back.

"Where you all headed?" asked the driver.

"LA," said Tink.

"Oh, LA huh? Yeah, sure. Right. LA."

Unlike the friendly Missouri sheriff, before long one asked, "How come you guys don't get haircuts? Are you draft dodgers or anti-American or something?"

"No, we haven't been drafted yet," said Gallagher. It was a worry for us though.

"Well, those peace marchers oughta be taught a lesson." The passenger took a pistol out of the glove box, waving it around but not pointing it at anybody. "America—love it or leave it, you know?" I wasn't sure what exactly he had in mind but the effect was each of us silently asking ourselves did we really want to be in that car with a gun-waving patriot. After a few minutes he put the gun back.

"Are you all hippies?"

"No," Gallagher said without elaborating. We called ourselves freaks, or heads. Like stone freaks or acid heads. "Hippie" was a newspaper word. To me it was like referring to indigenous Americans as Indians.

"You believe in free love?"

"I don't know much about it," I answered for all of us. I secretly wished I had more skills in that department, like our driver in Illinois had shown with the woman in the red car.

"You smoke a lot of marijuana too, I bet."

"No," said Jude, the quietest one of us. Not enough anyway, I thought.

In the front seat the two men became more belligerent and Tink got the worst of it. "Stop it," I heard her say. After a few minutes she snapped, "Get your hand off my leg."

She was tiny, but she was like those feisty little dogs that bark like they're gonna rip you apart. Soon she added, "Just let me out of the car."

"You want out of the car?"

"Yeah. Let me out."

"Let us all out," I said. It seemed like rattlesnakes might be a safer risk.

I wondered if they were going to refuse to stop, but they pulled half way up an exit ramp to drop us off. We started to walk back down to the highway but Tink stood where she'd got out. She was all fired up and as they drove away she decided to sing out a long defiant "Fuucckk yooooooooooou!" They hit the brakes with a screech and roared back in reverse. Jude and Gallagher scattered and I jumped over the metal guard rail into the dark of some tall weeds and brush to get out of sight. My entire focus was on the possibility of gunshots. At the same time I had a subliminal impression of a stirring noise nearby, not unlike a rattlesnake. It was more of a clairvoyant sensation. After a moment the car pulled away with shrieking tires and I vaulted back onto the asphalt, not sure if I'd really heard something.

"That got pretty heavy there for a while, ya know?" said Gallagher.

"You think they'll decide to come back?"

"They could. We gotta get out of here fast."

While we pondered what we'd do if they circled around, another car came up the ramp and stopped, a small nondescript four-door. In a panic we hustled into the rear doors from both sides, all four colliding and jostling in the back seat instead of politely getting into both the front and back from the passenger side. As the driver pulled away we excused our haste and mentioned we were in a hurry to get off the roadway.

"I noticed," he deadpanned.

We explained about the guys with the gun, and then he asked, "Where you all going?"

"We're going to LA," somebody answered.

"I'm only going to Tulsa. Where you from?"

"Chicago."

"That's pretty cool." His name was Chuck, a sandy-haired man in his late twenties with an Oklahoma drawl, wearing coveralls and on his way home. He said he worked the evening shift at the Green Stamps printing plant. After we talked some he proposed an idea.

"I got tomorrow off and I could drive you a lot farther than I can tonight."

"Yeah?" We four looked at each other.

"I live with my mom near Tulsa. There's a couple extra bedrooms, if you want to stay over."

"You sure it's okay?" we asked.

"I'll tell her you're my friends from work and I'm taking you to Oklahoma City in the morning." She had two spare bedrooms and Chuck would sleep on the couch.

"I'm ready to crash all right," said Jude.

"She's real proper and religious, so tell her you're married," he advised us before we got there. She might've been less than convinced when he showed up with four obvious teens who looked suspiciously unmarried, but we were polite and deferential guests. Yes ma'am this and yes ma'am that. Tink and Gallagher took one room and Jude and I took the other.

Next morning while Gallagher and I were washing up in the bathroom he asked, "So how'd it go?"

"How'd what go?"

"You and Jude."

"We just slept, is all. We didn't do anything."

"You're kidding." He grinned at me in the mirror. "Not us. We did a lot more than sleep." Maybe they'd been inspired by the runaway husband. They made a good pair, the elf and the leprechaun. I wasn't interested in Jude though, not that I was any great catch either. In my usual obliviousness I hadn't considered that there'd be any actual fooling around. I forgot to wonder how the same conversation went between the girls. Did Tink ask Jude with a wink and a nudge, "How'd it go?"

After Chuck's mom made us pancakes, we piled into his car and headed west. Along boring stretches of road we passed the occasional red Burma Shave signs in sets of five with their clever rhymes. After the first sign, a person couldn't help looking for the next one, and then the next, and then the punch line.

> *If daisies are...*
> *your favorite flower...*
> *keep pushing up...*
> *those miles per hour...*
> *BURMA SHAVE!*

Going through Oklahoma City Chuck indicated the highway signs pointing south to Norman, and said he'd been put in the funny farm there for a time. He didn't say why, and I felt sorry because he seemed like a good guy. When he had to turn around, somewhere out in western Oklahoma, Chuck gave us his phone number at work and his mom's phone number. "If you come through here again, call me. I might be able to give you another ride." I think a bit of our wanderlust had scraped off on him.

By our third night we were in a small Texas town about a thousand miles out of Chicago, once again angling for another ride. With our small bundles we stood by the roadside in the streetlight and the ambient glow from a service station, a diner, and some other neon lights and advertising signs. We weren't stranded out in the middle of nowhere like we'd been once or twice, as for example on the Oklahoma rattlesnake highway, and we weren't as desperate to get out of there. Then a car pulled onto the road shoulder behind us and some teenage boys got out. I never knew if a group like that would be friendly or unfriendly.

"You hitchhiking?" asked the leader, about my age.

"Yeah, we're from Chicago," Gallagher said.

"No kidding? Wow, that's a long way. How long did it take you?" They seemed like local guys interested in talking and I relaxed.

"Two and a half days so far," I said.

Gallagher and I told them about our trip, while Jude and Tink walked down the road a bit to try flagging a ride. There wasn't much traffic but all the same it wasn't long before a red convertible with the top down pulled over for the girls. After a minute Jude and Tink called to us. Gallagher started away, and the guy I was talking to cautioned me, "Watch out for those guys. They've been hanging around town the last few days, but they aren't from here."

I thanked him for the bit of advice and joined my friends. The girls had already told them we were going to LA, and they said they were too. These two didn't demand that one of the girls sit in front. We got into the car, me up front and the others in the back seat. We were off into the night, in a convertible no less, with the warm wind blowing our hair and the excitement of being on the move.

I don't remember their names now. We could call one Driver and the other Rider, although from time to time they traded places. Once we got moving at highway speed a steady whirlwind of leaves, dust, and grit blew up at us from the seats and the floor of the car.

"This stuff will all blow clear in a bit," Rider assured us.

"Yeah, this car's been sitting outside under some trees for a long time," added Driver.

"We found it in a vacant lot and stole it," said the other.

When we said we were from Chicago they said that they started out in Michigan. They knew each other from being in jail there together. I couldn't get too judgmental. They didn't act like they were out to hurt anyone and at least they didn't pull a gun out of the glove box. Maybe they were Butch Cassidy and the Sundance Kid. Westward across Texas we flew, joking and laughing and trading stories and cigarettes and now instead of a band of four we felt like one happy party. Six vagabonds without a care in the world, on the road going nowhere, wishing ill towards no one.

I felt safer with them than around so-called normal people and their insane world of vanity and greed, conformity and bigotry. For that I should go to Vietnam? No thanks. That kind of normal had produced the guys in Oklahoma with the gun, maybe even the disillusioned runaway husband. We were the sane ones—Chuck, the car thieves, and me. All we wanted was our freedom. We were looking for a way out of the rat race.

By morning they began to run low on gas. Driver said, "We're going to look around for a car we can siphon some gas from."

"We gotta be quick. It's best if you aren't along, in case we get caught," said Rider.

"We'll be back for you soon though." We didn't know if we really believed it.

They dropped us off on the edge of a town and we went into a cafe to get some takeout coffee to drink in the parking lot.

"You think we'll see 'em again?" wondered Jude.

Gallagher shrugged in answer.

No more than half an hour after leaving us, here came Rider and Driver all smiles in the convertible, and we cheered and waved because they had kept their word and come back for us. This time Jude sat in front with them. They were easy-going and cheerful, respectful, and didn't try any funny business with the girls. I wondered how they siphoned gas out of a parked car in plain daylight and halfway thought they might've sneaked off to buy gas and a good meal. If they were the criminals they made themselves out to be, or if they were just cautious and concealed their money and means from us, it made no difference to me. I knew their word was good about getting us to California.

In the afternoon the Arizona State Police pulled us over. Maybe six people in a convertible with out-of-state plates looked suspicious to them. I thought we were all in trouble, but after checking everyone's IDs they left the four of us by the roadside and ordered Driver and Rider to follow their patrol car. Speeding? Stolen license plates? Warrant? We were sorry to see them go.

We walked a ways down the road to a safer spot where someone could see us in time to pull over for us. Gallagher and I sat while Jude and Tink tried the passing cars for an hour. Could it be? Around the curve came our two friends in the convertible, honking the horn as soon as they saw us and waving, and the girls jumping up and down, we're all laughing as we pile into the car to continue our journey together. They didn't offer an explanation of what happened to them, but they kept their word and carried us on to LA

Somewhere in New Mexico we stopped for gas and bought sodas. When we got on the road again the girls started giggling because they had swiped some snack-size bags of potato chips. They wanted to impress the two guys, but the men had some advice for us.

"You might as well steal big stuff because you get in as much trouble for small stuff," Driver said.

"And another thing," said Rider, "don't do anything to get arrested unless you have enough to post your bail." Maybe paying bail is how they'd gotten turned loose in Arizona.

As we got closer to Los Angeles they let us know their future plans. "We're gonna steal a boat and go to Hawaii," claimed Rider. Now that was thinking big.

"You can all come with us," his friend said. They sounded pretty confident. I didn't pause to wonder how you steal a boat. What kind of boat would make it that distance? Did you just hot-wire one? And if you did, you'd have to know more about navigation than following a road map and some highway signs across the water.

It was a temptation and I knew he meant it, but we stuck to our plan. I wished Driver and Rider luck, hoping they'd make it to their tropical nirvana. With some reluctance we parted ways, us to see the Sunset Strip first, and then on to San Francisco, where I hoped to find peace at last.

CHAPTER 17

We hung around the Sunset Strip for a couple of days. The street people were as friendly as Wells Street in Chicago or Adele's Bar in Cleveland, but it was harder to find a place we could crash overnight, and it was impossible to get spare change from tourists. We didn't go into any clubs because we couldn't afford a cover charge. I had the similar feeling of being shut out that I'd felt in Greenwich Village, except here instead of crowded sidewalks on narrow streets we were on a wide boulevard with lots of traffic.

The one time anyone paid attention to us was when a neatly-dressed Japanese family with an infant arrived after dark in a Volkswagen bus. They wanted to recruit several of us who were lingering on the sidewalk to come with them to a Buddhist ceremony. It was nighttime and we were suspicious at first, but they seemed for real and promised to bring us back afterwards. They drove us to an ordinary residence where the main room was set up like a small temple with an altar and some cushions scattered on the carpeting. In front of the altar were fresh flowers and a platter of fruit that we wanted to eat but they smiled and told us it was for the ceremony. We took off our shoes and they taught us to chant Nam Myoho Renge Kyo, which we thought was lots of fun. Although they were polite and friendly, they didn't feed us and didn't know where we could stay. After an hour or so they brought us back to where they'd found us. It was all very LA. Nothing like that ever happened in Cleveland or Chicago.

I sent a letter to my family saying it had taken three days to get there, and by my calculations I had traveled 13,000 miles so far that year. I complained that southern California was the phoniest place I'd visited. I enclosed the sliver of paint that I had scraped from the Chicago jail cell to carry in my wallet, and included a Chicago address to forward any mail I might get.

After we were done with the Sunset Strip, somehow we all made it to San Francisco together. It was afternoon when we arrived in the Golden Gate Park panhandle. An outdoor concert was in progress and we sank onto the grass at the back of the crowd. Somebody said one of the San Francisco bands was playing. I couldn't see anything from where we were and was too exhausted to walk any further to investigate. People were passing around joints and we heard it was the day LSD was made illegal in California.[1] Between the pot and the long trip from Los Angeles I fell asleep and woke up as the afternoon grew late and the music was over.

The others had asked around and heard we could stay in Oakland at a commune called the Kerista house. We didn't know what Kerista was, other than it wasn't Nam Myoho Renge Kyo. It was on 38th at Telegraph, three miles south of the main Telegraph Avenue scene next to the Berkeley campus. We found a plain pinkish stucco house with a front porch, not much of a back yard, and a dilapidated garage to the side rear. It was some kind of commune that didn't turn anyone away, and we crashed on the floor there with a dozen other people.

Gallagher and I hitched a ride back over to Haight-Ashbury the next day. It was no glitzy Sunset Strip or Greenwich Village. No tourist shops or bustling night life. It was more like Wells Street, without the clubs or cafes. Only a hardware store, a liquor store, a small grocery, that kind of thing. The street was like any other street, so nondescript you wondered what was the attraction, why it was becoming a Mecca. The only difference was the people like us in small clusters on the sidewalks, or meandering as far as street's end at the supermarket and Golden Gate Park on Stanyan Street.

I sensed that the people weren't locals the way they had been in the other cities I'd been to. They were a friendlier bunch than in LA. They had made a deliberate journey here. They seemed more like pilgrims, like Gallagher and me. The things they carried: Zig-Zag papers, matches, guitar picks, incense sticks, alligator clips, faucet aerator screens (for hash pipes), *Berkeley Barbs*, spare change, peace buttons, feathers, bells, flutes, jaw harps, harmonicas, and patchouli oil. Some carried guitars, with or without cases. A very few carried sleeping bags or blankets. Nobody was organized enough to have an actual backpack.

The only thing noticeable about them were more guys with their hair down past their ears, some sprouting beards. Girls wore headbands or a few bead necklaces. Some people wore surplus olive-drab army jackets. Colorful clothes, marching-band jackets, the tie-dyes and bell-bottoms, all the fashions that the Sixties are remembered for were yet to arrive.

There was nothing to see on Haight Street, except for the Psychedelic Shop, which sold rolling papers and water pipes, books like *The Tibetan Book of the Dead* and Huxley's *The Doors of Perception*, and a few records. The first issue of the *San Francisco Oracle* was for sale. Some trippy instrumental music was playing and I went up to the counter to ask about it. The record was "Section 43" by Country Joe and the Fish, an EP that had been released in June. In the windows were announcements for Family Dog concerts at the Avalon. We would have gone but we couldn't afford the three dollars to get in.

The only other memorable places were the Foghorn Fish and Chips and a spectacularly disorganized toy store where we bought ice cream cones. The Haight Theater was boarded up and there was no inkling of the huge crowds that would materialize in the coming year for the so-called Summer of Love. As yet there were no tour buses, no one snapping photos or buying souvenirs. No dogs wearing paisley bandanas, no mental cases or police riots.

At the Kerista house a few evenings later, a meeting was convened to decide whether runaways should be allowed to stay. The discussion weighed the legal risks of harboring possible minors against the principles of the Kerista ideology, whatever that was. I didn't realize that Jude and Tink and Gallagher and I were the reason for the meeting, because I wasn't a runaway and didn't consider my companions to be runaways. No one asked us or we could have told them that we had already been checked out by the cops in Missouri and Arizona. A vote was taken among the Kerista members and the decision was that so-called runaways could remain. We left soon after anyhow, because we never had planned to stay. Jude and Tink phoned home for money to buy bus tickets to Chicago and were out of our lives. My court date to get back the bail money was near, so after about a week in San Francisco Gallagher and I started back too.

We headed south again, stopped on Sunset Strip, and then wasted a day hitchhiking down to Newport Beach. It was my first experience walking on the sand and seeing the Pacific. Gallagher and his family had lived there once, and he wanted to look up a girl he knew, but no one was home, so we set out to depart California. It took us hours.

Long after midnight we wandered the maze of greater Los Angeles. That late, it wouldn't do any good to stand at a freeway entry ramp because there were few cars on the street. There was so little traffic on the freeway that we thought if we stood on the shoulder it would be safe for someone to pull over for us. We clambered down a steep embankment covered in ice plant. The tangled stalks weren't as easy to walk through as they looked and I concentrated on my footing.

There was a crash of metal and sliding sound of tires on pavement, and I looked up to see two or three cars piled together not a hundred yards beyond us. The sudden noise was followed by the unreal silence that always seems to linger for a moment or two after a wreck, as if time pauses. I was already freaked out by the driving I had seen in the Los Angeles region. From where we stood, it was difficult to tell how much damage there was. I imagined severe injuries or bloody fatalities.

"Should we go help?"

"We better not hang around," Gallagher said.

Maybe it was our fault. We might have distracted someone looking at us or swerving toward the roadside to stop for us. A few other cars on the road slowed for the wreck.

"They'll be more help than us."

We scrambled back up through the ice plant, feeling guilty, and hurried to put distance between ourselves and the frightening scene we might have caused. I kept hoping it was a case of drunk driving and not because of us.

Much of the night we wandered streets and intersections, overpasses and onramps, with no clear idea where we were. By early morning we were walking a frontage road bordering a freeway and saw a well-dressed older man struggling with a flat tire on the narrow freeway shoulder. We climbed up the high chain link fence and dropped over to the freeway side to help. The flat was on the driver's side and several lanes of traffic were whipping by. The crash was fresh in my mind. While Gallagher assisted with the jack and tire iron I walked back down the road a ways and waved a bandana as a caution to drivers. When the tire was changed and tools put away we asked the man for a lift. He took us about ten miles to a freeway exit ramp and let us out.

"Thank you, boys," he said.

Er, ah, "Glad to help, mister."

Okay, well we had really been hoping for a decent ride, or at least some thank-you money to buy breakfast. Los Angeles. About as friendly and phony as the Sunset Strip. Were we surprised?

We crossed the road from the off-ramp to the on-ramp and got a lift with a guy who apologized ahead of time for not going very far. He found out we were going to Chicago and told us about an experimental nutrition supplement he was developing for camping and backpacking.

"If you boys want some to take with you, I'll give you a sample supply. It'll last you a few days."

"Sure. That sounds great."

"Yeah, we could use that."

Dropping us off, he pulled over to open his trunk and retrieve a quart-sized jar of it in a brown paper bag. It was a fine brown grain resembling wheat germ.

"Take this with you, and drop me a line from Chicago and tell me what you think of it." For some reason he neglected to give us an address where we could send our opinions.

"Thanks. We will." We walked to the next on-ramp. Within twenty minutes Gallagher fumbled the paper bag and it hit the pavement.

"Oops."

We picked up the bag to look. Broken glass was mixed with the food, so we left it with all the other garbage on the roadside.

"Smooth move, Gallagher."

A bearded Hells Angel in a Cadillac convertible with the top down pulled over on the freeway and Gallagher and I both got in the front seat, me in the middle.

"Hey, thanks man."

After a couple of minutes sailing in the heavy LA traffic he held out a smoldering joint. "You want a toke?"

"Oh, wow. Yeah."

"Yeah, thanks man," said Gallagher.

"I been holding this the whole time," he said with a grin.

"We didn't even notice," I said. After a good laugh at ourselves I took a puff and handed it to Gallagher. We passed it around until it was a roach too small to pinch in our fingertips and one of us ate it.

That night Gallagher and I stood in front of a green highway sign lit only by occasional headlights, where the eastbound road split outside of Barstow. Most of the traffic veered north toward Las Vegas. An occasional car continued on Route 66, across the Mojave Desert for 140 miles to Needles. It seemed likely we were going to be stuck there for hours. I was wrong though, and in a short time we caught a ride and were well across Arizona the next day.

CHAPTER 18

On Route 66 we blazed into New Mexico. A tribe of reservation Navajos in a station wagon stopped for us in the late afternoon. The back seat was filled with kids, so we shared the cargo area with their dog and a lowering October sun glowing through the back window. The Sandia Mountains stood bloodshot ahead of us, above a purple valley where Albuquerque's lights were beginning to kindle.

In twenty-four hours we'd come seven hundred miles, but we knew we wouldn't get another ride in city traffic. We had to cross town first. We bought sodas at a gas station and began trudging the sidewalk while the darkness came down. We were well into town when a voice behind us called, "Hey, wait," and I turned to see two girls sprinting towards us.

The one with long glossy dark hair launched a breathless opening line. "You go to the university," she said, pointing at me. It was a statement more than a question and I had to grin. We didn't know we were just then walking past the University of New Mexico nearby.

To be agreeable I said "Okay."

"Do you, though?" she asked.

"No, do you?" She looked kinda cool.

"No, we live here. We were in a restaurant and saw you walking by." I was charmed that they chased us down. The dark-haired one with deep brown eyes was Toni, and the skinny blonde was Marlene.

We said we were hitchhiking to Chicago. "We started out in LA yesterday."

In the neon light from a window we stood and talked a while, smoking and getting better acquainted, while the girls appeared to gauge where we fell on the spectrum between helpless kittens and psycho killers.

It seemed an opportune moment to ask for food. "We haven't had anything to eat all day. You think you could maybe get us something?"

Marlene invited us to her house. "My dad is there sleeping. He won't wake up if we're quiet."

We walked to a residential street, and slipped into a darkened house and followed Marlene to the kitchen. She reminded us again about her dad and we spoke in low voices while she made us peanut butter and jelly sandwiches. While we wolfed them down with glasses of milk, she made us each another one.

They admired our long hair and said it would look better if we washed it, if we wanted to. I was feeling pretty grungy all over so I said okay and Marlene got some shampoo and towels. Gallagher and I took turns over the kitchen sink, and then the girls decided to help, getting their hands in our hair, shampooing and rinsing us. After they toweled down our heads pretty well we all started in flirting.

The girls grew more and more bold. Someone got specific with, "Who's going first?" We tossed a coin and Marlene and Gallagher went to the bedroom nearest the front of the house. I was kind of relieved to wait, not real convinced about this situation yet. While Toni and I sat in the kitchen I began falling into the deep trust of her friendly brown eyes. Being alone with her settled me down and I was more at ease than in the group commotion. The others came out and we took our covert turn in the darkened room. I was so beguiled that I could have remained there. They weren't kidding about New Mexico being the Land of Enchantment.

. . .

Gallagher and I had to get going. "Take us along," they said. That's how it was all across the country, restless kids everywhere itching to kick loose from monotony and get somewhere lively.

How old were they?

"Sixteen," said Marlene.

"Fifteen," Toni said, "but I'll be sixteen next month." Oh great. I thought they were closer to our age. I hadn't exactly asked for a photo ID when we were waiting in the kitchen. The three-year difference between us was criminal from the law's point of view, even if those girls weren't previously innocent. Crossing state lines would really up the ante. I had a vague knowledge of the Mann Act, that we could be arrested, like Chuck Berry. Didn't he spend time in prison for the same thing just a few years before? It was a big risk but I liked Toni and wanted her to come with me. We all four walked back to Route 66 to hitchhike together.

A few hours later it was still dark and we were three hundred miles east, outside of Amarillo, Texas. Two guys stopped for us, a cowboy in a hat and a salesman in a loosened necktie, both pretty hammered. They'd been at a roadside bar and decided to get a couple of six-packs and keep drinking after closing time. While we motored eastward they shared some beers with us. They were out cruising they said, and eventually would have to turn around and go back to the salesman's car in Amarillo. It was still parked in front of the bar, and if we rode back with them, he'd take all four of us to his next stop somewhere further up the highway. We all agreed it was a good plan.

We drove for an hour and then turned around. We got back to the salesman's car all right. He opened up the passenger side of his car, crawled in, and right away toppled over with his head on the driver's side under the steering wheel and passed out. It didn't look like he'd be in shape to drive anytime in the near future. The cowboy wasn't in better condition but drove away in his own car. We wished we'd gotten out when they turned around. Maybe fifty or sixty miles we had gone and come back and now we had to make up that distance all over. I still wanted to put a lot more miles between us and Albuquerque.

It was just getting daylight and I saw the salesman's wallet had fallen on the seat when he keeled over. I contemplated my moral qualms, and Gallagher resolved the impasse for me when he grabbed the wallet and pulled out a wad of bills. The girls hadn't seen, and we hustled them onto the highway. The plan was to hitch a ride before any cops happened to come by. I was afraid if they investigated the man passed out in his car, he'd send them looking for us.

Within minutes a car with two guys in the front seat pulled over and the four of us crowded into the back.

The two guys in front took turns asking each other, "Is the bar open yet?"

"Nope, not yet." We asked what they meant and they said the bars were closed until a certain hour, and they had to hold off drinking until the legal time. We continued to drive along, into the sun breaking over the horizon.

"Open yet?"

"Nope. Twenty more minutes." In the back seat Gallagher took out the bills and counted. It was seventy-five dollars, a fortune by our standards. In the front seat, the two men were unsuspecting.

These past few days from Chicago and back on Route 66, we'd encountered men with guns, hitchhiked in a stolen car, seen a freeway wreck, met Hells Angels, underage girls, and drunk cowboys. Taking a man's money seemed to fit right in. In the wide open spaces on this side of the continent, you could lose your bearings. Poetry and the mimeo revolution were somewhere behind me and it seemed uncertain that I'd get back to those civilized shores.

"Now is it open?"

The passenger looked at his watch. "Yep. Bar's open." From under his seat he took a fifth of whiskey in a brown paper bag and broke the seal. He drank a swig and passed it to the driver and then around to all of us.

The Texas highway seemed like one long drinking and driving road rally. People lived by their own rules out here and it wasn't hard to revert to a lawless Wild West.

· · ·

By the end of the day we made it to Tulsa. We phoned Chuck, the guy we'd met only a couple weeks before on our trip west, and he came to get Gallagher and me and our new girl companions. His mother was away so he took us to stay at her house again. That evening he made up his mind to take us all the way to Chicago, and the next day quit his job at the Green Stamps printing plant. He had to wait a few days to collect his final paycheck so we stayed and lived on the seventy-five dollars.

Chuck drove us out to some mountains one night where we could park and walk some easy trails to an overlook. There was no one else out there. Toni and I sat with him high on the bluffs and studied the view in the moonlight. Gallagher and Marlene disappeared and we didn't know where they went until we got back to the car. It wasn't locked but we found them huddled in the smaller space of the trunk, trying to stay warm. Gallagher was shivering. He hadn't been feeling too good and now he was getting worse. Back in town we took him to an emergency room where a nurse checked him out. She left the room for a few minutes to get something and the enterprising Gallagher told Marlene to look in the cabinets for some syringes to steal. He wasn't doing any hard drugs then, didn't even have any. He thought in Chicago he'd find some use for hypodermics or at least be able to sell them. There were some in a drawer and Gallagher pocketed a few. I didn't like where this was going.

Chuck's mom was due home, so he took us to stay at his brother and sister-in-law's apartment. It was one of those shabby cinder block places where all the rental units are joined together in a long row with a view of the highway. We bought some Vicks inhalers that we broke open to eat the cotton inside. It wasn't much, just enough to make you feel a little alert for a while. The next day he got his paycheck and cashed it, and we hit the road in his car. We all had money now and could stop sometimes to eat.

"Wait! Listen." Through the intermittent crackle on the radio caused by power lines, we heard "...pickin' up zzzurrz vibratiozzz" and "good good goommm ...brations." It was the new song we'd heard only a couple of times in the week before. Toni was in the front seat and adjusted the tuner and turned up the volume. We were in awe. In spite of the Beach Boys's sappy falsettos and chorus-boy vocals, the total effect of "Good Vibrations" put my head in a different space. It wasn't a song. It wasn't music. It was a kaleidoscope.[1] There was no other term for it but psychedelic. Radio stations played it for the rest of our trip and it put a spell on me every time.

CHAPTER 19

I had about 16,000 miles behind me after we got to Chicago. Toni and Marlene split and did their own thing most of the time, not always with Gallagher and me. But Toni was okay to hang out with and I saw a lot more of her after Marlene took a bus back to New Mexico. On Wells Street we met a guy named Dusty who wore a denim Hells Angel jacket, a chain on his belt, and motorcycle boots. He had a beard and uncombed hair as long as mine. You didn't see Hells Angels outside of California.

"How come you're in a place like Chicago?" I asked him.

"It's for the movie *The Wild Angels*. They're paying me to stand outside movie theaters for publicity."[1] It didn't seem like a very Hells Angel thing to do and I wondered if he was for real. But whether he was or not, he fit the part, and he was friendly to us, as friendly as the Hells Angel that picked up Gallagher and me on the LA freeway.

"Let's get some wine," Dusty said. He was old enough to buy.

While we walked to the liquor store, Toni told Dusty and me about some modeling she did for a photographer. You couldn't tell from her looks she was fifteen, and she signed a paper saying she was eighteen.

"What? With your clothes off?" I said.

"No. He gave me different costumes. He said he was going to pay me, but all I got so far were copies of the pictures."

In the store we went over to a floor display of straw-wrapped bottles of red wine. "So when's he going to give you your money?" Dusty asked, swinging a wine bottle up by the straw handle. It broke and the bottle thudded on the linoleum floor. Even with the straw padding it cracked and a puddle of red wine spread out.

"Hey!" The excited store keeper shouted and came rushing over with a mop, frowning like we did it on purpose. "What do you think you're doing?"

"The handle broke, man," said Dusty. "It wasn't our fault."

We paid for a different bottle and got out of there. In a quiet alley we passed around the wine and Toni showed us a stack of black-and-white snapshots in which she wore some modest costumes the guy provided. None of them were too exotic.

"He said he'll pay me more to take my clothes off, but I'm not going to." It wasn't clear to her if he was going to give her the money he'd promised for the first shoot. She had the prints, that's all. She gave me one I liked, where she looked straight into the camera, wearing a short fringed poncho of rough burlap-looking fabric.

Dusty said, "I'll go over with you and make the guy pay up." It must have made an impression, Toni showing up with a Hells Angel. She got her money.

I was going to get some money too. I had a court date that I intended to keep, to get back the bail money that Gallagher and Jan had put up for me.

The night before my scheduled court appearance, Pepper sold Gallagher and me some acid. It was some of the first acid for either of us, or possibly the very first. We dropped it and waited around on Wells Street to see what happened. After about thirty minutes it started to take effect, and we could tell it was going to be different from other stuff we'd had.

"Come on," Gallagher said. "We gotta get our money back."

"What do you mean? I think, uh, I think it's working."

"Yeah. I know. We got to get our money anyway." We were getting to the last of our funds and Gallagher was going to cheat Pepper.

"I'm starting to space out, man." This wasn't feeling like pot.

"Hey, maintain." He meant act like we weren't affected, while we were still able to do so. "You gotta maintain, man."

"Gee, I don't know, man."

"C'mon."

We found Pepper in the crowded Stage Coach Restaurant at North and Wells. He was sitting in a booth by the window with two other guys and we went over to stand next to the table.

"That stuff's no good, man," Gallagher said. "You gotta give us our money back."

"What? That's good acid," Pepper said.

"No it ain't," said Gallagher. "Nothing's happening." Everything in the Stage Coach looked fake to me. The tables and seats and dishes looked like toy play sets, the walls were a hand-painted temporary backdrop. Somewhere hidden behind all the fake scenery was a real universe that all the mixed-up man-made clutter blocked from view.

Pepper looked at me and said, "C'mon, Randy. You know it's good."

I said, "I don't think it is." A juke box murmured far out on the horizon. The nearer background sounds of clattering dishes and humming voices were movie sound effects.

Gallagher stayed focused, holding out for our money while the floor dropped away and the ceiling lifted. Pepper stalled, and then finally wavered and gave Gallagher the money and we left before the whole illusion collapsed like soggy paper. My hair was flaming with showery sparks.

We were up all night, sitting in doorways or stopping in at crash pads to stare wide awake into space. At dawn we were a few blocks from Wells, over by the shore while the sun rose over Lake Michigan. Pepper was right, this was really good stuff. It was gentle too. The thing is, we could function just like normal, but saw things you wouldn't usually notice.

. . .

Gallagher and I walked to the Cook County municipal courthouse, still tripping. Into the tall building we went, got into a crowded elevator next to uniformed cops and other people who pretty much paid us no mind. I was certain that we emitted a bright blinding aura that everyone could see. It seemed impossible that they didn't notice the dazzling glare and clamor radiating from our heads. We struggled to maintain, to blend into the norms of everyday behavior, but on acid you realize nothing is normal or everyday, that people go to great extremes to pretend it is, such as dressing like cops and elevator operators and attorneys.

We found a courtroom, possibly the correct courtroom, large and crowded, a vast hall with rows and rows of folding theater seats. The tall windows had rollup shades pulled down to keep out the direct morning sun, casting a golden glow over the room. Throngs of people milled about in the central aisle. A continuous parade was coming and going in the side aisles. Indistinct murmurs from the judge's bench in front were obscured by the shuffling of feet and the sound of doors opening and closing, people coughing and whispering, opening satchels, exchanging papers. I couldn't figure out a pattern or a protocol. By now the acid had mellowed out enough that I was capable of standing before the judge while tripping and pleading not guilty to whatever the charge was, loitering, or walking on the sidewalk, or whatever Lieutenant Aguado had accused me of. It was hopeless though. Neither of us heard my name called. The pandemonium in the room was unending and after an eternity I gave up and we left without getting the bail money. There were just as many people when we left as when we arrived.

Back on Wells Street we looked for Chuck. He'd bought himself a black French beret and a bright green shirt made out of some satiny material, a flashy spade style you'd expect to see someone in the crystal-meth crowd wearing. He was wearing new dippy-looking Beatle boots. Maybe to someone from Oklahoma it was cool. Between ourselves, Gallagher and I disapproved. We didn't tell him we were tripping and Chuck loaned us his car so I could drive Gallagher to his parents' house in the suburbs. I wasn't daunted by the drive through Chicago streets. The acid gave me hyper-control and awareness of traffic. I had the sensation that I was steering a mythical chariot and my hair was wild snakey Medusa flames. No one was at the house and we ate sandwiches and took baths and washed our clothes. By the time we got back with Chuck's car we were coming down, and went over to Sedgwick to crash.

Stealing the salesman's money, stealing the syringes, cheating Pepper. It wasn't cool to be ripping people off. That's not where I was coming from, even as hard up as I was. I knew I should have objected, too. Not saying anything made me just as guilty. Gallagher was getting to be a bad influence. Now that I was hanging out with Toni, I didn't have as much time for him, and we gradually parted ways.

CHAPTER 20

I picked up my forwarded mail, including a government letter stating that I had to report for a draft screening. I'd registered my address as an inconspicuous crossroads town in remote northern Wisconsin, near where both my parents were born and raised and where they settled when my dad retired from the Air Force. My theory had been that all the local eligible and clean-cut sturdy farm boys eager to serve their country would increase my own chances of being rejected. It was the same flawed reasoning that had made me claim once that I wasn't a Nebraska resident.

I went because if you didn't do it the Feds supposedly hunted you down and put you in prison. I bought a bus ticket to the town, Prentice, where a military bus would ferry me and all the country boys to an inspection center in Minneapolis. We were to be thrown into the meat machine like so much beef in the stockyards. On the bus I sat alone behind the driver, not talking to anyone. In that small community I supposed everyone else already knew each other and I let them wonder who the weirdo in front was. My out-of-place long hair and wire-rimmed glasses helped. I put an unlit cigarette in my mouth and let it hang there. I wanted to arrive in Minneapolis with the general perception that I was a basket case unfit for the military.

A year ago the radios were playing Sonny and Cher's "I Got You,

Babe." The song this year was Bob Dylan's "It Ain't Me, Babe." The mess over in Vietnam had nothing to do with me, and so many prominent voices opposed it that I knew I wasn't wrong.[1] I couldn't picture myself in a crewcut and military gear, hanging around with a bunch of gung-ho mesomorphic types, oiling a rifle and doing pushups. I didn't want to wear a uniform. If some guys wanted to play Boy Scout, I didn't object to them doing so and it wasn't up to me to prevent them. I accepted that the world had always seen war. I just didn't want any part of it and I didn't want to obey orders. "Obey" was a four-letter word. All I wanted was to stay clear. I was sorry for other guys like me, unwilling to go but with no way out. It was a bad situation of everyone for himself.

After a three-hour ride the bus brought us to a hotel for the night where we were fed dinner, dessert included, served on actual plates at a table. The last time I'd eaten meals like that were at the fraternity dinner for Allen Ginsberg in Lincoln and the spaghetti restaurant in Denver. Afterward they started pairing us up for rooms and a guy came over and said he was my cousin John, and did I want to share a room? He'd been on the bus and I guess he found out we had the same last name. I only had a hazy notion who he was. I had thirty or forty cousins in Wisconsin but since I didn't live there I had relatives I'd never met, or only met once. I took him up on his offer and after we found our room he invited me along to a movie with some of his friends. I didn't have money to spare for a movie, so I declined and stayed in the room to enjoy a warm bath and a clean soft bed, like a cowboy fresh off a cattle drive.

The next day we were fed a real breakfast—more luxury—and went to the examination center, joining other busloads of teenage boys from all over the region. In asbestos-tiled, fluorescent-lit assembly halls we were herded into neat rows for roll call. By this time I had detached myself from my cousin so I could focus on being unacceptable. I was behind enemy lines here and needed to stay vigilant. It was American to resist. The way I saw it, my patriotic duty was to defy conformity. The way the government saw it, it was subversive.

I tried the tactic of hanging a cigarette off my lower lip again and some crewcut draft center guy in white pants and a white shirt noticed and said, "No smoking!"

"It's not lit, man."

"Take it out anyway. It looks dumb."

My first mistake was that I complied. I wasn't in his army and shouldn't have taken orders so readily. No need to make any of this easy for them. I should have lit it. I should have yelled "No smoking!" and grabbed a fire extinguisher off the wall and leaped onto a desk, fogging the room bazooka-like, screaming, "Kill for peace!" But anything too extreme would get me arrested and jailed and I wanted to avoid that.

We all stood in our underwear for the physical exam. It might've helped my cause if I hadn't worn underwear, but since I did, I should have thought to wear some lacy women's lingerie. Another missed opportunity. A doctor sauntered past us, inspecting each guy. He peered at my feet and said in a speculative voice, "Flat feet?" I was hopeful, willing to be waved out of line and dismissed. Maybe he was teasing me, because he apparently decided they weren't flat enough to disqualify me and moved on.

Dressed again in our clothes, we filled out questionnaires including a section about criminal records. I guessed being rounded up for loitering in Chicago wouldn't have been serious enough and wrote that I'd been arrested for burglary. One at a time we took our forms to people at desks who looked them over. The woman screening my papers confirmed a couple of facts with me and then hesitated when she saw the section about police records. "Did you go to jail for that?"

I figured they could check it out anyway so I said, "No, they changed it to petty theft and the charges were dropped." That wasn't true either, but it sounded believable, like the kids in Chicago who got caught shoplifting the salt and pepper.

"Oh dear," she said, making a correction in red pencil. "You shouldn't have put that on there then." She didn't want a little hiccup like burglary to eliminate me. It was such a great honor to be drafted.

I just hadn't prepared very well for all the ways to get kicked out.

Unlit cigarette, borderline flat feet, criminal tendencies... My final hope came when I was sent over to wait on a bench along the wall. They didn't say what for. I figured it was for suspected perverts.

I thought, *Great. This is where they conclude I'm unfit for duty.*

A higher ranking fellow came over and the attendant gestured to me and said, "What about this guy?"

Yeah, you guys don't want a degenerate like me.

But the big shot just said, "No, he's okay," and I didn't get to stay on the Reject Bench.

Jeez, are you just blind or what?

When we left the center they handed each of us a miniature New Testament. A reminder I guess, that America had God on our side. I tossed it somewhere before we got on the bus. On the ride back from Minneapolis I again sat alone, thinking about how I hadn't done enough to keep from being drafted. With the government, the army, the war all pressing in on me, the truth of the matter was it was giving me a bad case of pre-traumatic stress disorder. Would I flee to Canada or just go to prison?

We got in at dark and the local boys dispersed. A few might have lived in town, others had a ride waiting, most drove away in cars and pickup trucks they had left there the day before. While everyone cleared out, my cousin asked if I needed a ride and I said my family was coming for me. They weren't there to meet me so after it got quiet I started walking west on the dark and deserted two-lane highway hemmed in on either side by the northern woods.

Above me the galaxy set up a clamor. No lights of civilization contaminated the clear sky and the stars were so numberless that a person could see by the shine of their combined brilliance. They looked almost close enough to reach up and touch. They hadn't changed since I'd first visited my grandparents here as a child. I had the feeling they were speaking kindly to me, if I could only hear their voices. I strained to detect a message, something wonderful that would free humans from history's troubled ignorance and allow our souls to live in peace. How was I going to get to higher consciousness in this monkey world of activity, avarice, and aggression?

After ten or fifteen minutes my mom and sister cruised up in the gas-hogging luxury-model Detroit iron my parents always preferred. It was the first and only car on the highway and I knew it was them when I saw the headlights. I climbed into the back and they took me to the rented farmhouse they'd occupied since leaving Nebraska.

There weren't any warm fuzzy feelings or huggy moments. We were never like that. My sister admired my hair and soon after we arrived my dad got home from his new civilian job. I felt uneasy seeing them all again after a year and half. Imagine the talk when we sat down to dinner...

"I sure miss those times when dad shook me until my head jerked," I said, buttering a roll. "Those were the good old days, huh?"

He chuckled and said, "When you got too big for spankings, I had to use the belt on you. I must have punched you in the chest, because there was one time when you couldn't breathe."

"Yeah, I remember I couldn't get air in and kept making funny wheezing sounds," I said.

My sister reached for the salad dressing and joined in the merriment. "I remember when he hit you and your glasses flew on the floor and the frames broke."

"Oh, that's true. I'd sort of forgot about that," I said.

"You had to tape them together so you could wear them," she elaborated, passing the green beans.

Now mom contributed some family nostalgia. "Remember when I threw a fork at you?" she asked. I was nine years old then.

"The tines stuck in my chin, and it just dangled there," I reminisced. We all laughed hearty laughs over mashed potatoes and pork chops.

"I remember that too," my sister chimed in. "I was sitting at the kitchen table and she was chasing you and you dodged the opposite way."

"It sure was comical," I said, wiping away a sentimental tear. "Dad, that's while you were in the Philippines." I still didn't know that some parents actually appreciated their kids.

"There's butterscotch pudding for dessert," mom said...

While all those things were true, we didn't really have that conversation. So what else was there to talk about? They didn't seem to disapprove of me trying to stay out of Vietnam. My sister was in high school and excited about my exploits and poetry achievements. I'd sent her some of my poetry printings and now I told her about my party for Allen Ginsberg and Karl Shapiro in Lincoln, about giving poetry readings with d. a. levy in Cleveland, about the freight train from Denver, and sleeping on rooftops in New York. It was enough for her to regale her friends later, while they conspired to be cool despite being stuck in a little burg.

The couch was made up for me to sleep on. In the morning after some breakfast my dad drove my sister to school and took me to where the Greyhound stopped on its way to Chicago. While we waited he gave me five dollars, like Mr. Simon had on the Fourth of July. It wouldn't begin to get me through MIT.

I had only come because I was in the area and it was what you do, I guess. I wouldn't see them again for thirteen more years, but I kept in touch with an occasional letter or phone call, so they'd know I hadn't died.

CHAPTER 21

November was turning Chicago cold. Now that the draft physical was done, I wanted to go back to San Francisco and bring Toni with me. I considered the two choices, Route 66 or straight west. Even though it meant having to go to Los Angeles before heading north, Route 66 was familiar to me, and Toni too. I decided that with Toni along it would be easier for us to get rides on the shorter route by way of Lincoln. Easier than when I had tried it alone.

In Lincoln we went to the SDS house where Tim and I stayed when we came through on the freight train from Denver. It was still something of a crash pad, though nowhere as crowded as places I was used to seeing. The first morning a clean-cut boyish-looking guy stuck his head in the room where we were still laying under a blanket.

"Hey man. You haven't seen Richard come by lately, have you?"

"No. We just got here last night. We're on our way to San Francisco."

"Oh yeah? Well if you happen to see him tell him Channing is looking for him."

"Channing. Okay sure. I know Richard from when I lived here."

"You lived here? What's your name?"

"Randy."

"Are you Randy Rhody?" That surprised me.

"Yeah."

"You know Darlene, right? She's talked about you. I'm Chan, short for Channing."

"Hiya. I thought Darlene was in New York." I hadn't seen her since we visited the Peace Eye Bookstore.

"No, she's here." She and Chan had met in Chicago and together they had come to Lincoln. "I'll be back later and take you to see her."

Darlene was at Judy McClanahan's. She admired how long my hair had grown and she and Judy and Toni got the idea to entertain themselves by putting it in pigtails. They had a laugh at what a great job they'd done, and then added some hair ribbons. They decided to take it a step further, so I allowed them to put lipstick on me. They thought the result was such a riot that they did up my eyelids and eyelashes, then added some face powder. They penciled on a beauty mark. A pity they weren't around when I had my draft physical.

I couldn't see what they were doing but Judy's boyfriend George watched this transformation with mixed expressions of revulsion, fear and fascination. I don't think he was as horrified at me for allowing them to beautify me as he was at himself when he began to realize that he found it attractive. The girls wanted me to put on some female clothing. I drew the line and flat out refused, and I sure didn't try to imitate any feminine mannerisms either.

After I judged they had all admired their handiwork long enough I went to inspect the result in the bathroom mirror. I didn't study myself for more than a few seconds, because it was too weird to look at. I quickly scrubbed my face clean of all their artwork and undid my hair. When I came back out they seemed a bit disappointed, except for George. He looked relieved.

A couple nights later Darlene and Chan and Toni and I were at the apartment of two other girls we knew. They ordered a pizza for delivery and I looked forward to it, famished as always. We didn't have anything alcoholic or to get high with while we waited around for the pizza to arrive.

"Did you ever try Asthmador?" asked one of the girls.

"What's that?" I'd never heard of it.

"It's a powder you burn, for asthma. It has belladonna in it, that's kind of poisonous if you eat it, so it makes you have hallucinations."

If it was cheap and legal I wanted to see how it compared with grass and acid and Vicks inhalers.

"Someone else has to watch and keep you under control, in case you do weird things."

Chan and Darlene and Toni and I decided to experiment and see what it was like. We didn't know how much to take, and each scooped a teaspoonful from the tin box and washed it down.

By the time the pizza arrived the belladonna was starting to take effect. As much as I wanted to eat, when I took a bite I couldn't chew or swallow, and it felt like I was choking. I could hardly breathe. Pretty soon Chan stood up with a distant stare on his face and removed all his clothes. "Chan, what're you doing?" His mind was far away and he wouldn't answer. He marched with purpose to the bath-room and started filling the tub, then climbed in and sat there in a trance. Soon after, I was a walking zombie too, completely poisoned.

It might have been a hallucinatory, only the wrong kind of hallu-cinatory. The next day Darlene remembered going out in the street and talking to the fire hydrant, thinking it was some misshapen little man. Luckily a watchful escort had gone along with her. Our sitters said I had sat at the kitchen table and kept looking down in my lap thinking I had dropped a lit cigarette, when there was no cigarette. I had some dreamlike after-images of that. I had a vague memory of lying on the bed with my back to Toni and she was clawing at my back, making my nerves and spine shudder with chalkboard-screeching electricity. The rest of the night was a blank to us, more entertaining to the watchers. We all agreed belladonna was horrible. Maybe the key was to take a much smaller amount. I concluded it wasn't something I'd try again.

· · ·

I hoped to put together some fake ID for Toni, so we went to the public library and got her a library card. She didn't have to pass for twenty-one to get around the country safely, only eighteen. A library card was a start. Even if it wasn't the most believable, it gave us the illusion that her identity was already transforming, and we'd soon add more corroborating documents. It wasn't clear yet what that might be. I only had a driver's license myself, an expired student ID, and my old 2-S student draft card.

One of my old friends, Frank McClanahan—he was Judy McClanahan's brother—had replaced Steve Abbott as editor of *Scrip*. The previous year we'd sat in Steve Abbott's apartment and got into a debate about who was a greater writer, James Joyce or Baudelaire, and made it into a poetry-writing contest—sonnets, limericks, haiku, whatever. Frank would write something on behalf of Baudelaire and read it to me. I'd compose something in favor of James Joyce and read it to him. Dueling poems. It made more sense to me than political argument.

Now he said, "Wow, you're like a campus legend." I didn't ask what he meant by that, because I couldn't imagine being more than a vague memory to two or three people. I hadn't done anything legendary that I knew of. I was still writing poems in a new notebook I'd gotten to replace my lost Record of Mishaps, and even though I wasn't a student any more, Frank wanted some of my poems to put in the next issue of *Scrip*. I never knew if he did, because it was the last time I was in Lincoln, and soon Toni and I were on our way again.

The morning that we got out to the highway west of Lincoln, we almost immediately caught a ride in a semi truck going to Wyoming. The driver said there was a bunk behind a curtain in the rear of the cab, where one or both of us could crawl into and nap if we wanted. I'd never seen a sleeper cab. It might have been quite comfy, though I didn't climb around to look. We could tell he was a decent guy, but we didn't know him and out of caution we declined.

The days were shorter and long after dark we came to a major truck stop in Wyoming. The driver was going to take a break and invited us to come along as his guests to a separate rest area for truckers, instead of the public diner. There wouldn't be any trouble with other drivers, he said, and it was real comfortable and even had showers. In those places, the truckers may have been mostly family men, and there might have been a woman driver or two. It was another unknown to me. The world was so full of pitfalls that for my part I imagined an ominous crowd harassing me about my hair and making remarks at Toni. We decided to wait in the truck.

He was going to turn north further up the road and would have to let us out there, so he located another trucker inside who was going further west and was agreeable to taking us. They came out to the truck and he introduced the guy as Red. Red seemed trustworthy and we transferred to his truck.

Later at night we stopped again and got out to use the restrooms and stretch. We made it quick. The flag at the Little America truck stop snapped and blew straight out in the freezing mountain wind. We were glad to be in a heated truck cab. In the morning he too turned off onto another route and had to let us out.

The sun was up but it was still cold. We weren't getting good rides and I eyed a slow-moving freight train with open boxcars going our direction right next to the road. I halfway wondered if we could jump it but for Toni's sake I decided not to risk one of us getting seriously hurt or killed. We walked and got short rides, walked and got short rides.

By mid-afternoon it got real discouraging and there wasn't a lot of traffic. A green MG with the top up pulled onto the shoulder ahead of us and we hurried to see where it was going. A well-dressed black guy on the heavier side with a mustache, maybe 35 or 40, was on his way to California. It was just a sports car with bucket seats but he said we'd both fit in the passenger seat if Toni sat on my lap. A couple hours later I took over the driving so he could get in a nap. He seemed pretty safe and Toni was okay with sitting on his lap, and in fact they both slept while I picked up the speed through Utah and into Nevada. When he woke up he remarked at how much road I'd covered.

Across Nevada and California overnight we came down into Oakland and got to the Kerista commune by morning. Kerista wasn't even as roomy as the Chicago crash pads, just three rooms downstairs with wall-to-wall sleepers at night, and a small private room or two upstairs. The front room was furnished with an old beat-up sofa and small cots, where everyone sat around in the evening passing joints. Toni and I relaxed and got stoned with them.

After a while I noticed one guy lifting his ankle with his hands as if to assume a lotus position, only he sat frozen halfway like he'd forgotten what he was doing. I glanced away so as not to stare and next time I looked he still held his leg in midair, immobile and not speaking to anyone. He seemed catatonic the way I remembered Julius Orlovsky. Or else meditating, or paralyzed in an acid trance. After that I often noticed him sitting motionless for so long that I got tired of waiting for him to move. I wondered what sort of mental state it would take for me to sit rigid like that. I don't think I ever heard him speak more than a word or two. It weirded me out and I avoided him.

Another guy was Jimmy, cool, not creepy. He was a red-haired, red-bearded guy about average height, of indeterminate age who could pass anywhere from late twenties to forty. For a meth dealer he was nice enough. He had a regular business going, usually in the empty one-car garage out back, where sometimes I watched his customers, including lots of Hells Angels, pay him to cook up speed in a spoon and tie off their arms and give them a hit. One evening after dark a black guy and his girlfriend came by the house. They looked like a presentable straight couple going on a date to the movies. He gave Jimmy some money for two hits of speed and Jimmy shot them up in the front room where we were all smoking dope, the guy first to make sure it was good and then his girl, and they left. Nobody in the room paid much attention. This wasn't exactly the San Francisco destination I had in mind.

If someone with a car was going over to San Francisco, Toni and I could catch a ride with them. If not, we were just a block from MacArthur Boulevard, a busy thoroughfare we could hitchhike on that fed straight onto the freeway crossing the Bay Bridge. We stood in front of Hy's Restaurant and Cocktail Lounge at MacArthur and Telegraph, often in the rain. When I sent my family the Kerista house address to forward my mail I enclosed a matchbook cover from Hy's that I labeled "Official Souvenir." I was expecting my draft results to arrive, and they did. My new status was I-A, meaning available for military service. If there was one piece of ID I didn't want, this was it.

CHAPTER 22

On Haight Street it was still a fairly quiet scene. We walked past a long-haired guy about my age leaning against a wall who asked if we wanted to buy some pot. We couldn't afford any but we started talking. His name was Ron. We told him we came from Chicago and were staying in Oakland. He told us he was from Denver. After a while he asked if we wanted to get high and we went to his place, the spacious first floor of a Victorian on Cole Street. He shared it with a wan-faced guy with stringy blond hair who looked as malnourished as me, and a straight-looking girl with a cast on her leg, getting around on crutches. There being no furniture in the house, we all sat on the checkered black-and-white kitchen floor to toke on a couple of joints Ron passed around.

In the past month, after arriving in southern California from Chicago the first time, I'd covered about 6,000 miles to San Francisco, back to LA, up Route 66 to Chicago, a detour to northern Wisconsin and Minneapolis, and then west to San Francisco. The grand total since June was about 19,000 miles. For a while Haight-Ashbury seemed like a peaceful haven where I could restore myself after months of homeless searching.

We stopped in at Ron's often. He still had one bedroom that wasn't occupied and Toni and I wanted to rent it, only we didn't have enough money. All we needed was a *pied-à-terre,* and we could work on an eventual upgrade. I asked if he'd rent us the many-windowed back porch until we could afford to rent the spare room, and he said for ten dollars we could have it.

After Toni and I left and walked down Cole we passed a garage built into the front of the house at street level. Through the open door we saw half a dozen mattresses stacked against the wall and a middle-aged black man moving some boxes around inside. We asked if he'd sell us one of the smaller mattresses and he said we could have it for five dollars. We told him we'd be back, and went down to Haight Street to panhandle enough to pay for it, splitting up on opposite sides of the street to ask for spare change. I asked anybody, even one woman who looked like the last person who'd want to give money to street people, and she surprised me by giving me a handful of change, almost a dollar. I was glad to be in a city like San Francisco where people were generous. In less than an hour Toni and I had our money and went back to pay for the mattress and we carried it up Cole Street to our back porch.

We ran into George from Lincoln, who'd given me the poster scraps that I used for my *4 Suits* poetry book. He said Pat was also around, my old roommate from W Street where we had the party for Allen Ginsberg. George told us they'd nearly been swept up by the police during some riots on the street. They were sleeping at night in Golden Gate Park. It was already raining more days than not, and I gave him our address on Cole.

We headed over to the nearby Panhandle Park to see about a meal after someone handed us a leaflet announcing free stew at four o'clock for anyone who brought their own bowl. It was a small gathering at first and in no time we got to know two of the organizers, Emmett Grogan and Billy Murcott. They called themselves the Diggers. They made a daily stew in ten-gallon milk cans at various kitchens, sort of a Meals on Wheels for the street people. Once or twice they used our stove at Cole Street. Emmett and Billy and one or two other guys—Peter Cohen[1] might have been one—came by in the morning with their cans and collection of produce and whatever meat they had for the day. We all smoked dope while we chopped vegetables and got the cooking started. In the late afternoon they carried the milk cans out to a VW van for the short trip to the Panhandle.

We were having stew in the Panhandle on an overcast day and a school bus painted in bright colors drove by on Oak Street, people standing up through an opening in the roof and waving and cheering. Later it circled back the other way on Fell.

"What's that?" I wanted to know.

"Ken Kesey's bus," someone said.

"Who's Ken Kesey?"

"He wrote *One Flew Over the Cuckoo's Nest*. He started the acid tests." I hadn't read the book and I'd missed out on the acid tests by arriving too late that summer. Tom Wolfe's *Electric Kool-Aid Acid Test* hadn't been written yet. It may have been Neal Cassady driving the bus, except at that time I hadn't read *On the Road* either, so I didn't know who Neal Cassady was. Even Emmett Grogan wasn't widely known. No one was trying to become a legend or the subject of books and movies.

The seeker in me wasn't looking for perpetual indulgence for its own sake. I wasn't looking to be a prankster or to wear flowers in my hair, wasn't marching to Timothy Leary or chanting Hare Krishna. Maybe others were looking for an endless Mad Hatter tea party. Not me. With Toni I hoped to settle in some place and resume my poetry and my greater quest for enlightenment of some kind.

The Diggers set up a big window frame in the park that they wanted everyone to walk through before they got their dish of stew. It was a street-theater piece they called the Frame of Reference, as part of their involvement with the Mime Troupe. A performance group of actors didn't interest me as much as poetry did. We heard later that they took the frame up to Haight Street and got arrested for being a public nuisance.

Toni and I gave Billy Murcott the name Curly Bill because of his long dark curly hair that stuck out from under his cap. We knew some other Billys and we had to keep them all straight. He seemed okay with our name, but I don't think he usually went by that. Sometimes Curly Bill came by our place on Cole Street with a joint or some hash to pass around. He showed up one night with a telephone company handset he said a lineman had given to him.

"He just gave it to you?"

"Yeah, I explained to him about the Diggers and he said here, take this." People often helped the Diggers in weird ways like that.

We went outside in the dark to clip it onto a phone line next to a house, to see if we could make a free phone call. He must have been connecting it wrong because it didn't work, but next time we saw him he said he'd been able to make a bunch of calls for some other friends.

Emmett and Billy were setting up a Free Store in a garage on Page Street. Toni and I and several others helped them carry out junk and sweep it clean. Maybe by that time we ourselves qualified as Diggers. Why not? There were no admission ceremonies or papers to sign, no dues to pay other than the contribution of our efforts. Unlike SDS, this was more the kind of organization I could associate with, a non-organization.

Right before Thanksgiving Emmett and Curly Bill rounded up some of us to go to the supermarket at Haight and Stanyan. They had a handful of newspaper coupons good for a free bag of potatoes if you made some purchase that qualified. They got a couple of turkeys and other Thanksgiving groceries and divided them up among us all to buy separately, and gave each of us enough money and a coupon so we could pay for our portion and also get the potatoes. Between several of us we had a haul of potatoes big enough for Thanksgiving as well as enough extra for some of the daily stews.

On Thanksgiving we went over to the Page Street garage. The serving tables were old doors laid across sawhorses and crates, loaded with turkeys and potatoes and the whole Thanksgiving spread. It was cold and rainy outside and going dark, and we ate standing up or sitting in a few wooden chairs scattered around without tables. At least the lights were on and our mostly destitute friends were gathered.

We'd been in California about three weeks when we went to the Panhandle for stew as usual. Billy was there with the *San Francisco Chronicle*. It had a front-page headline and story, and a large photo of Emmett and some others I didn't know on the steps at the Hall of Justice. The public nuisance charges for the Mime Troupe window frame incident on Haight Street had been dismissed. It was a good picture too, and we thought it was fun to see that our friend was notorious.[2]

In addition to the Digger stew, we usually panhandled money to buy hot fish and chips. As December came it rained often. The wet night-time pavement twinkled with a Christmas glisten of reflected street lights and headlights, tail lights and shopfront lights. Toni and Billy and I were walking on Haight Street one of those sparkly wet nights when two policemen on foot confronted us and asked to see every-one's ID. Toni of course didn't have any, and said it was at the apart-ment. They must have heard that excuse hundreds of times. They put her in a squad car and drove her over to Cole Street to get it, while Billy and I walked the few blocks there to find out what would happen. I was alarmed. I knew all she had was the library card. If we had thought of it, we should have asked the Diggers to get her some believable ID. Too late now.

The police car was parked in front and we went up the steps and knocked at the ornate bevelled-glass door. George Eade opened and told us we better stay away until all was clear. The cops were in the back, he said. In the mist of an intermittent shower we walked out of sight and waited. When we returned the squad car was gone and we went in to hear the news. The cops had allowed Toni to gather up a few of her things and taken her to Juvenile Hall up by Twin Peaks, where Market Street becomes Portola Drive. The next day Billy took us in the VW van to find out what they would do with her. Not being relatives, we couldn't actually see her, or I would have gone every day and I didn't. All we could get was her status. Her future was uncertain and we had to wait many days to find out.

Eventually we learned that Toni was being returned to Albu-querque, where I first had met her. She had an older brother there, over twenty-one apparently, and she would be released into his custody. At the Kerista house I spread the word that I had to get down to Albuquerque. Two people, Ken and Jeanne, were driving to Los Angeles in a couple of days, where Ken was going to drop off Jeanne and then drive back to Oakland. They took me south and left me in the late afternoon at a crossroads where I could hitchhike east to Albuquerque. By nighttime I made it as far as Barstow, dropped there when my ride turned north in the direction of Las Vegas. I was going straight east through the Mojave Desert on Route 66 and found myself trudging through Barstow late at night. With the lack of traffic, it felt like a vacant side street. In the headlight beams I could see the misty drops of a light rain that was beginning to fall.

Miraculously, a car stopped and I dashed to the open passenger door and climbed behind the forward-tipped front seat. It was no clunky family sedan. It was a Ford Mustang, or a muscle car of some sort, or anyway a car built like a lean mean street machine. As I got into the back I saw the two guys in front were longhairs.[3] I was so grateful that I exclaimed, "Wow. Heads!" They said they were going through Albuquerque and lit up a joint and passed it around. I even-tually settled back in a marijuana haze and fell asleep. In the morning we stopped in Arizona someplace for coffee and gas and pressed on. Later in the day they dropped me off at an address I had in Albuquerque, only a few blocks off the highway as it went through town, adding another thousand-plus miles to my travels.

CHAPTER 23

Toni's brother Matt lived with Tanya, a waitress who was away at work during the day. They were expecting me, but not exactly with a genial welcome. After letting me in, Matt huddled down on the carpet with a Mexican blanket over his shoulders, in front of a large sheet of artist's paper taped to the fake wood wall, and resumed working on a drawing with black ink. He seemed much older and not very interested in meeting me. At least he was an artist and not a square office type or a bull-necked blue collar bigot. Snow was on the peaks outside Albuquerque and I was satisfied just to be in from the cold.

Bleak, low-angled December light came into the basement apartment through narrow windows high up near the ceiling. A haphazard exhibit of unframed poster-sized drawings were taped onto one wall —Matt's art work. Each completed drawing was a full-page outline of a human head in two-dimensional profile, every one a different shape. But shape was all they had, no recognizable human features such as ears or hairlines. Inside the profiles he had traced convoluted mazes, whorls, clusters of dots, and abstract patterns, with the density of an Albrecht Dürer woodcut. Every drawing was unique.

During the next day or two I didn't see Matt do much of anything except draw and play Ravi Shankar records. He had a faraway look and in a different way he was as freaky as the suspended-animation guy at the Oakland Kerista house. He didn't just hurriedly dash off his drawings. On the second day he paused to contemplate his current work-in-progress, looked at me, then studied his graphic further, looked at me again, and proclaimed, "That's you!" It was his usual labyrinth of lines that had no resemblance to what could be called a portrait in the usual sense. He might have considered it a street map of my soul, or just as easily a sinister spell. He continued working on it and I took it as a positive sign that he accepted my presence in spite of ignoring me most of the time. While Matt worked I sat on the floor too, there not being any chairs except at a kitchen dinette set, and scribbled aimlessly at poetic verses or read a book and smoked.

When Toni was transferred from San Francisco, she was held for a couple of days while processing through some authoritarian mumbo-jumbo. Tanya took me in her car to visit. After Toni's release Matt didn't suddenly begin acting like a dutiful older brother. Tanya was the practical-minded big sister to all three of us, a role she seemed more resigned to accept than pleased about.

We didn't stay with Matt and Tanya for more than a day. It wasn't clear to me if Toni had been living with them or some other place the night in October that Gallagher and I first came through town. Her friend Marlene was back at home with her dad. Toni knew a lot of local people, some only enough to visit, some who gave us temporary places to stay.

After a few days we alighted at a crash pad in the form of another basement apartment that was rented by a woman named Bernice who worked during the day. It seemed to be a shelter and crossroads for a mixed population of bikers, dealers, longhairs and heads, but it wasn't my idea of a permanent haven for us. There was no Haight Street in Albuquerque, there were no Diggers, and we didn't have a back porch with a mattress to sleep on. We couldn't risk trying to hitchhike back to San Francisco. We lacked a plan.

· · ·

Chuck blew in from California in his little tan car, still wearing his goofy beret, bringing along Ken, the tall guy from the Kerista house who'd driven me to LA at the start of my trip to Albuquerque. Ken had a new companion, a small Hispanic girl named Maria. The three of them had followed my trail to Albuquerque and now they camped at Bernice's along with Toni and me and other remnants of the dope-smoking crowd.

We were in need of food and funds. Chuck had a little gas money and not much else. As we grew more desperate he broached that we break in somewhere to steal money. Except for the groceries I took in Cleveland, I'd never committed a real burglary and wasn't crazy about the idea, but I didn't have a better one. After midnight he and I drove around for a while until he pulled into an alley behind a small darkened burger joint in an area that wasn't busy with cars.

"This looks like a good place," he said. As senior conspirator Chuck took the lead. "Wait here behind the wheel while I go in."

"Shouldn't I come along?"

"No, keep an eye out. If anyone comes, drive away." He got out and took a tire iron from the back while I slid behind the steering wheel, relieved to stay with the car and be the getaway driver. All was quiet and deserted while I waited in the cold with the engine off. I didn't hear any sounds coming from the building, or see any lights come on. After about ten minutes Chuck came to the car with two large cardboard boxes that he put in the back seat.

"I've got another one inside," he said. He went back and returned with the other box and got in. "Okay, let's go." I started the car and drove off.

"How'd it go?" I asked.

"I didn't find any money," he reported. "I got some frozen hamburgers and some cheese and buns though."

"It's something to eat anyways." I was disappointed that he hadn't found a pile of cash, but he'd done his best, which was more than I could say about myself.

"I got a stereo set too that we might be able to sell." I wasn't interested in having to fool with selling stuff but I kept my mouth shut about it.

At Bernice's we fried cheeseburgers for everyone. We ate burgers for the next few days and Chuck wired the receiver and tuner and speakers together. It wasn't safe to try to sell the stereo equipment yet.

"They'll probably be reported stolen," he said. "Better to try and unload them later in some other town or another state."

With Toni two years away from turning eighteen, a library card from Lincoln hadn't kept her immune from police. We thought we could legally go back to San Francisco with Chuck if we got married in Mexico. On Christmas eve, Chuck, Ken, Maria, Toni, and I drove south through Texas to El Paso and crossed the border into Ciudad Juárez. We felt like outlaws finding asylum, as if we'd forded the Rio Grande on horseback with Texas Rangers galloping in pursuit.

At first we walked around Juárez taking in the seedy aspect of the streets, unsure where to go. I tried to practice my Spanish on some mustached taxi drivers leaning against their cars, without much success. None of them knew where we could get married. They asked if we wanted to buy marijuana, but we were certain it was a police entrapment and politely declined.

We'd brought along a good-sized piñata that someone in Albuquerque had given us after we said it would make some kids in Mexico happy. Our chance came when we went into a tiny cafe with about three or four tables, where the owner made us rice-and-bean dishes on a kitchen stove in the rear of the room. We were the only customers. Her small daughter was with her and we called the shy little girl over and gave her the piñata as a Christmas gift.

After we ate we found a burlesque club, the sort of place we couldn't go into in the United States. Here we could walk right in and order a pitcher of beer, Toni included, no questions asked. Two unshapely dancers in sequined bikinis took turns swaying on stage. Aside from us there were a couple of patrons sitting at a bar, and a crowded table of cowboys who said they drove down from Montana.

If there was typically a boisterous crowd from El Paso in the place, this night they had dispersed for Christmas rituals and family gatherings. The forlorn atmosphere didn't put me in a mood to celebrate. We couldn't afford to order ourselves more than one round of beer and left.

We resumed walking about, looking for a cheap room for the night. A slick-haired Mexican in a suit and a bolo tie and polished cowboy boots attached himself to us, all friendly and polite and conversational. I was suspicious and uneasy. In English he asked who we were and where we were from, and tagged along as far as the front door of a small hotel where we left him and went in. For three dollars an old woman rented us a double room on the second floor, divided into a front and back area, each with a double bed and bare wood floors. The room had no heat and an unshaded light bulb dangled on a cord from the ceiling. It didn't come with a TV or a clock radio. The communal bathroom was in the hall.

There was no lock on the door so we blocked it with Chuck's bed in case the well-dressed Mexican came looking for us and brought some shady friends. We didn't have a good idea how to share the beds, so Chuck slept alone and the rest of us crowded the bed in the back area, girls in the middle. The bedding was thin and worn. The foot of the bed frame collapsed from our combined weight and we had to get up and put it back together.

Christmas morning was sunny and cold. We heard a rooster and out the window saw chickens in the bare dirt next door. Chuck thought someone had tried the doorknob in the night, but with the bed against it, it couldn't be forced and whoever it was had gone away. We left the hotel and Toni and I went to mail a post card. Not far from the hotel we went into a tortilla factory and watched two or three people at work making and bagging tortillas coming off a conveyor. For a few pesos they sold us a kilo in a paper bag to share with the others.

We didn't know how to go about getting married. I was expecting some kind of neon-lit marriage chapel like I heard they had in Las Vegas. Near a church we saw a padre on the street and stopped him to ask if he could marry us. He said no, which kind of ended our flimsy plans.

We needed money. Chuck had the idea to sell our blood in El Paso, so we recrossed the border and slept in the car that night. On Monday at the blood center the screening nurse asked me if I had hepatitis or had been around anyone who had it. I remembered that while I was waiting for Toni in Albuquerque, I'd gone with some people to visit a guy who was staying in bed at his parents' home to recover from hepatitis. Just being in the same room was enough to disqualify me. The donor center took Chuck and Ken's blood, for whatever the going price was, but the money they got wasn't much. Chuck phoned his mom in Oklahoma collect and she wired him additional money for gas to drive back to Albuquerque, no better off than when we'd left.

CHAPTER 24

I was feeling ragged, like I might be getting a cold. At Bernice's apartment a biker guy gave me a few loose pills that he said would help the symptoms. For all I knew they were over-the-counter cold pills. I swallowed a couple and wrapped two or three in a piece of tin foil to carry in my pocket for later. We talked about the draft and he said there was a drug called Ritalin, used on hyperactive kids, that would give you heart murmur symptoms for the draft physical. I had no idea where I was going to find Ritalin but it was a piece of advice I would try if I got a chance.

Toni said that besides her brother Matt, she also had an aunt in Albuquerque. On a sunny day between Christmas and New Year's Chuck loaned us his car so I could take Toni for a holiday visit. When we got to the house her aunt invited us into the living room and Toni introduced me. Before we even sat down there was a knock at the front door and her aunt opened it to two middle-aged men in suits and hats. Toni and I withdrew into the kitchen, thinking they had some business with the aunt. I whispered to Toni how they looked like Lyndon Johnson, which was not a compliment. But the joke was on us. They were plainclothes cops who had followed us from Bernice's apartment.

They checked our IDs and went through our pockets and found the pills I had wrapped in foil, and then took us out of the house without handcuffs. It wasn't clear what they wanted us for. One took Toni in their unmarked car, and the other one made me follow them in Chuck's car while he rode on the passenger side. I turned over in my mind some possible escape ideas—ram the other car from behind, or suddenly brake and jump out of the car and run. I knew neither idea would get me very far.

At the police station they separated us and I was allowed a phone call, so I called Bernice's apartment and told Chuck what had happened and that the cops had his car. I was put in a holding cell alone and after about an hour an assistant DA and some other men came to ask permission to search the car. I refused. I didn't know what, if anything, they would have found incriminating, but it wasn't my car, and if they wanted to search it they could ask Chuck.

They left and after another hour I was taken out and escorted to a small office where a fat man sat at a desk. I assumed he was a judge. Seated in a semi-circle facing him were Chuck, Ken, and Maria to my left and the Lyndon Johnson cop who had arrested me on the right. I took the empty chair front and center, confused that it wasn't a courtroom, and there was nobody to read me my rights, no court-appointed attorney, no court stenographer. I noticed my pills in the opened foil wrapper sitting on the judge's desk but no mention was made of them. I didn't know what to expect, hoping this would go the way it had in Chicago, that time when the judge said, "English and anthropology," and let me go.

He began asking me questions. "Where are you from?"

"Lincoln... San Francisco."

"What are you doing in Albuquerque?"

"Visiting Toni and friends. Traveling around, just seeing places."

"What do you do for work?"

"Some temporary jobs." I didn't get specific about working for Add-a-Man in Chicago or mention that I was a wandering poet. It would have been an excellent time to produce that newspaper story from Cleveland, the one with my poem and picture, or a copy of *Paracutes*. I should have had those papers from high school graduation that said I was a Regents Alternate and Nebraska University Honor Student and stuff.

He questioned me for five or ten minutes and my impenitent demeanor probably didn't help my cause. He could not have been happy about working over Christmas break. I faced an old warthog who needed to show some rebellious kid he was boss.

It came out of nowhere, unexpected. "Sentence is thirty days in county jail."

What? But what for? Ken and Maria and Chuck looked on silently. No one said a word. I remained mute and was taken away. I never heard what the charge was, or what the pills were, whether they were over-the-counter or prescription. Was it legal for them to enter the aunt's house to seize us, and why were they even following us in the first place? As destitute as I was, and if they were competent, they couldn't mistake my presence in town for some kind of illegal dealings, a stranger involved in big drug or marijuana sales. Good thing it wasn't the wild west and he wasn't a hanging judge.

Chuck and Bernice came to see me in a long room where visitors faced prisoners through thick glass windows. Using the telephone handset, Chuck reported that Toni was in juvenile custody and that he had retrieved his car. I told him I'd been asked about searching it and we agreed the best thing for him to do would be get out of town. We said goodbye, and I never saw him again.

As I was being led out of the visiting hall a Mexican guard nudged me and handed me an unopened pack of cigarettes and a book of matches. He pointed to another prisoner in the visitor area, close to my age and about my height with thick hair combed back like a greaser, in black jeans and motorcycle boots. He nodded and I motioned with the cigarettes as a gesture of thanks.

Early the following morning a guard took me from my small

holding tank to an expansive cell that housed about a dozen guys. The prisoner who'd given me the cigarettes wasn't among them. A few sinister-looking Mexicans seemed to dominate the cell. I usually liked Mexicans but these were unfriendly.

The jailers brought an oatmeal breakfast, and three Anglos about my age beckoned me over to eat at one of the metal tables bolted to the floor. They looked pretty lame, not like guys I'd normally hang out with. "Watch out for those Mexicans," one said.

"They'll beat you up just for fun," said a second.

"Yeah, they'll block the camera behind the mirror so no one can see them doing it."

Over the sink at the end of the cell was a mirror. It was probably metal, and not a one-way mirror. Were these guys putting me on?

"The ones who know they're going to prison are the tough guys. They want to have a reputation before they get there."

"They'll rape you too."

One pointed out a fat middle-aged American in a dirty white T-shirt sitting at another table. He seemed to get along with the Mexicans.

"That's Tex over there," the first one said to me. He didn't look like a Tex to me as much as a fat slob.

Another of the Anglos calmly said to me, "I married Tex last night." That stopped me cold. I didn't ask what exactly he meant by "married." He didn't seem all that traumatized about it, but I was definitely not going to marry Tex or anyone else. I thought of Mary Mary that night in Chicago. These boys didn't sound like they'd join together with me for mutual protection. I had to think of a way to get out of there, even if they carried my body out boots first.

Then the fun began. A guard brought a stool and put it inside the cell door and there was some banter between him and a couple prisoners as he locked the door again. The guard passed an electric clippers through the bars to one of the Mexicans. I saw where this was going. The jailer was going to let the prisoners do his job for him. The one with the clippers first gave a couple of his friends a trim. Then two of them grabbed me and marched me over to the stool.

Since there was only one way it was going to end, I didn't see the point in struggling. It would just make it more entertaining for them if I resisted. I hadn't cut my hair for a year and the guy with the clippers gave me a crewcut in a matter of minutes. Haircut aside, I was desperate to get out of this cell where Tex lived, so when the guard came back for the clippers and stool I asked to speak to whoever was in charge. He went away and I sweat it out, wondering if he'd be back.

In a little while he returned and took me out of the cell and escorted me to an office where an older Hispanic man in a uniform and a badge sat at a desk. I requested to be put into solitaire and he asked me why I wanted to be moved. He knew perfectly well about the haircut and the kind of men in that cell. I didn't talk about them though, knowing if they heard about it and I was put back in with them I'd pay for being a snitch. I made it sound like it was all about me, made some repentant sounds about my mistaken ways and how I just wanted to think about reforming. He told the guard to put me over in the women's section, which turned out to be a deserted separate area of four or five one-person cells where there weren't actually any women in custody. I happily spent New Year's Eve alone in my private cell.

I was no Charles Starkweather, yet in some odd way I felt like I deserved jail for leaving a trail of mayhem across several states. Convicted for stealing groceries in Ohio and milk bottles in Colorado, for robbing the salesman in Texas and stealing hamburgers in New Mexico. Guilty of consorting with dubious characters in stolen cars, of leading Toni and Chuck and others astray, and in general of leading a wastrel existence. Incriminated for being nineteen and wanting to be me and not someone else's idea of what I should be.

After the crewcut episode I was wary of everyone. When a trustee offered to take my clothes for laundering I thought it might be a trick. There weren't any jail clothes to wear, just what I'd been wearing the day I was picked up. He finally persuaded me that it was okay, and while I showered and wrapped myself in a blanket to wait, my laundry was done and everything brought back to me as promised.

I practiced Spanish with the Mexican jailers and trustees who brought my meals. I realized most guys weren't as vicious as the first prisoners I met and relaxed a little bit. They were all pretty friendly and sometimes they would sneak me an extra roll or something else to eat.

A guard came to get me and said I had a visitor. He took me to a private interrogation room, where the plainclothes Lyndon Johnson cop who'd busted me sat at a table. He motioned me to the other chair and offered me one of his cigarettes, a trendy new menthol brand with a plastic tip in the filter, aptly named True. Naturally a cop would smoke something called that. I took one even though I didn't like menthol smokes.

It still made no sense why they had staked out the crash pad and followed us. As far as I knew they didn't stalk anyone else there. He said, "We were watching that place you were at. We could have come in any time you two were in there together, but we waited until you were outside."

His point might have been that Toni was underage, but so many people hung out there that he was wrong to think he'd ever find us alone. I didn't say anything to support or deny his assumptions and he didn't press me for more details. Instead he inexplicably went off on a bizarre, outright psycho description of his own sexual vigor. I didn't know what he expected me to say to that and made no reply. I should have recommended he speak to Tex, since he seemed like a version of Tex in a cheap suit. I waited until he changed the subject and asked if I knew of any drug dealers, which I did not. He asked about a break-in at the little burger place the week before, and I said we'd been in Mexico the week before. Nevertheless I was glad that Chuck was gone. I hoped he'd taken the stereo and got some money for it.

A few days later I had another visitor in the same room. A man in a suit showed me his FBI badge and invited me to sit. He had a Tyrolean-style hat on the table, and his demeanor was congenial, friendly in a way that the cop was not. He told me I wasn't in further trouble, he'd just been sent to verify my whereabouts. The draft board was looking for me and he had to confirm that I wasn't available. I was apprehensive thinking how the draft had me cornered now. I confirmed that yes, it was me in the flesh, and no, I wasn't going anywhere, and he left.

No women were ever brought in, so they didn't have to move me. I guess they used the area for overflow because occasionally a male prisoner would be brought in and put into one of the other cells for a day or two. One night after lights out a jailer brought in a Mexican and locked him in the cell across from mine. They were arguing and the prisoner was demanding a blanket. The guard told him, "Shut up. You don't get a blanket." It was a personal punishment, not official, and we all knew it.

It was plenty cold at night even though I slept fully dressed under my blankets. The guard looked at me. "Don't you give him a blanket or I'll take away yours too."

A few minutes after he left us, the prisoner called across the passage to me, "Come on. Pass me one of your blankets."

"I can't. You heard what he said. I would otherwise." And I would have.

"Give me a blanket, I said."

"No. Sorry."

"If you don't give me a blanket I'm gonna beat you up tomorrow." Our cells were locked at night and in the morning the doors were unlocked and we could mingle in the small passage between the individual cells.

"I can't do it, man." I wasn't looking forward to a fight, although the guy didn't seem as mean as he talked. I hoped he was bluffing and wished there was a way I could help him. The guard came back and shined his flashlight in to make sure I hadn't passed a blanket over and went away again.

The prisoner unrolled all his toilet paper and spread it over the hard metal bunk platform for a cushion, and crawled underneath his thin mattress to use as a cover.

"Can you give me your toilet paper?" he asked. The guard had only mentioned blankets, so I passed the guy my toilet paper. He unrolled it and spread it under himself with the other roll and we went to sleep. In the morning when the lights came on I saw he wasn't as ominous-looking as the Mexicans in the big cell had been. Right away he said he didn't really mean it about beating me up. We got along okay and salvaged the toilet papers and rolled them back up. The next night he got two blankets and the day after that they took him away.

I spent a couple weeks in the women's area and most of the time I was the only person there. I was perfectly happy being alone. A uniformed guard named Bustamante brought me books that another prisoner sent over to me, a cellmate of the guy who'd passed me the cigarettes. A lot of them were the kind of books I would have picked to read anyway. One of them was the *Tao Te Ching*. I read a line in it that blew my mind:

Those who know don't tell. Those who tell don't know.

It was one of those statements like Allen Ginsberg had said to me, about shaking hands with a cloud. It seemed to be another faint clue to a mystery I couldn't quite define, let alone solve.

I figured whoever was sending these books must be a pretty good guy. Each time I finished and returned them via the guards, they brought me more. A couple of times the guards asked me if I wanted to move to the group cell where he was, but I thought about the cell where I got the haircut and the kid married Tex, and said I liked it where I was.

I was about halfway through my thirty days by then, mid-January. I didn't know it, but right about that same time my old friends the Diggers were putting on the first Human Be-In in Golden Gate Park.

Turns out Allen Ginsberg was there for that too. He was everywhere, it seemed. If Toni and I had still been there, we would certainly have been involved helping get it together, handing out announcements on the street, setting up the stage, maybe meeting some of the bands. We'd missed out on some cool things.

Bustamante brought over the guy with the books, Bill, to stand outside the main doorway and talk to me through the bars. The guards weren't supposed to do that and he took a personal risk bringing a prisoner over, not that Bill was dangerous. In fact, he loaned Bustamante comic books. He looked more studious than criminal, unremarkable in everyday clothes and short sandy hair and plain glasses, in his mid- to late-twenties. He'd come to ask me about moving over to the group cell where he was. I was suspicious about conditions there and asked if there were any troublemakers like the cell I'd first been in, and he said it was peaceful and everybody there was cool. I didn't have any belongings to take except for a couple of blankets, so I brought them and walked over with Bill, escorted by the guard. The jail blankets were not what you'd call luxurious. They started you off with two, but I'd gotten another one from a guy who'd been locked up in the women's area with me, and when I got to Bill's cell there was a spare blanket in the vacant bunk I inherited. The more blankets you could accumulate, the better.

The rectangular cell was the same as the other group cell I was in, looking about forty feet long and twenty feet wide. Along one of the long sides was a steel wall where an upper and lower row of bunks hung head-to toe, six on the top row and six below. The side opposite the bunks was made of steel bars, with steel tables and benches next to them. Beyond the bars there were translucent chicken wire windows that let in a gray light. The cell door was on one of the narrow ends and at the opposite far end was a toilet and a shower stall. The floor was plain concrete.[1]

All together there were twelve men in the cell. Bill had been in there so long that he had the position of seniority, front bottom bunk closest to the door, which is to say farthest from the toilet, and I saw that he had several boxes of books underneath his bunk. I met Carl, the guy who'd passed me the cigarettes in the visiting area. He was from Hartford, Connecticut and had been on a motorcycle road trip. A cop stopped him and found a lid—an ounce of pot—in his saddle-bag. I don't know what Bill was in for, or how much time those guys were serving. With the three of us, a couple other guys formed our regular group—Gary, a straight-looking Anglo like us, and Spider, a fortyish Mexican who could roll two cigarettes simultaneously, one in each hand. Whenever someone was released, that man's bunk was up for grabs if anyone wanted to move, and one by one our group gradually migrated forward so our bunks were all together in front next to Bill.

It had turned out to be a pretty good rest for me—three meals a day, a place to sleep, friends to hang out with, books to read. At the end of my thirty days I was released, and gave each of the guys one of my blankets. I asked Bill and Carl if I could do something for them outside, but Bill said he didn't need anything. Carl gave me an address in Hartford where I could get in touch with him if I got to the east coast.

Tanya took me to see Toni, who was awaiting transport to her parents in New York. No telling why she hadn't been sent there from San Francisco in the first place instead of to her brother. Why they didn't send her to New York immediately this time wasn't clear either. But here she was, still in Albuquerque, and by now she'd been held longer than me. When she finally was sent, I left town and started hitchhiking. I had her parents' address and phone number in Manhattan where she would be, and when I got there I could find her.

On the road again, and in February most places had some snow on the ground. There was one memorable ride, somewhere in Indiana, in a Jaguar sedan that pulled over to the road shoulder and took me on. The man's wife was Asian. You didn't see a lot of Jaguars, especially not out there in the hinterland. Or Asians either. They were on a long trip and took me hundreds of miles while I mostly just slept in the back seat. I wasn't much more trouble than an extra suitcase. One time they stopped for a break at a restaurant and brought me in with them. We all sat at the counter and the man bought me pie and coffee.

They dropped me off in New Jersey somewhere. It was night and snowbanks were plowed high beside the icy driveway of a Howard Johnson's. I stood at the YIELD sign where cars exited the parking lot, waiting for someone going into Manhattan to stop for me.

PART IV

NEW YORK

CHAPTER 25

I didn't have a Plan B. I was gambling everything on one address, a third-floor apartment on East 9th between Avenues B and C, in the same brick tenement neighborhood where I'd stayed in July. Even if I could have remembered where that crash pad was, all those people would be long gone. Now it was nighttime in the middle of a New York winter. Give or take a few days, it was a year since the February party for Allen Ginsberg in Lincoln.

When no one answered my knock I sat down with my back against the wall to wait as long as it took. The narrow hallway wasn't much warmer than outside, but it was dry and there was a light. I studied the opposite wall and waited for a girl named Cher. I didn't care for the idea of ambushing someone I'd never met outside her door and wished I had a better plan.

An hour or two later I heard someone coming up the stairs. A girl about my age with light brown hair appeared at the corner and gave a startled flinch when she saw me. I wasn't much of a threat sitting on the floor and she hesitated long enough for me to say, "Hi. I'm looking for Cher." Some random weirdo wouldn't know her name.

"Who are you?" she answered.

"A friend of Grady Waugh and Joe Knight from Nebraska. Somebody said you'd know where they are."

"Oh." She took a tentative step forward after recognizing their names and judging me to be pretty harmless. "I've seen them. But I don't know where they are now."

"I'd sure like to find them. I just hitchhiked from New Mexico and don't have a place to stay."

"There's some guys across the street who might know. I'll take you over there and you can ask them."

We went out and crossed over the icy sidewalk, snowbanks plowed between parked cars, and slushy tire tracks in the street, to a darkened storefront. As we got near I made out some dim candlelight inside and Cher tapped on the glass door. It wasn't a business, just a vacant space where two guys were living, more or less camping out. They had seen Grady and Joe Knight around, but didn't know where they were. It was encouraging news anyway. They said I could hang out there until we found my friends, and Cher went back to her place.

With that eerie feeling New York gave me of crossing into the nineteenth century, the aura of candle light on their faces made me think of two young soldiers who'd stepped out of a Civil War tintype. Danny was from Chicago and David was a native New Yorker from Queens who'd been to Chicago the past summer, where he'd met Danny. All the times I'd been through Chicago, I hadn't met either one of them. We started comparing who we knew from Wells Street, including Nick the telephone saboteur, and my freight train companion Tim, and Dirty Ralph and Friendly Fred. I told them I'd just come from Albuquerque, and about my travels in the previous months.

David made some tea while Danny strummed an out-of-tune guitar and sang "You Got To Quit Kickin' My Dog Around." The floor and stamped-tin walls were bare and the rest of the room was pretty empty. There were some boxes of used books that they had salvaged, after being abandoned on the sidewalk by a book store down the block that went out of business. The only identifiable furnishings were towards the back, a couple of mattresses they slept on and a rough wooden display table left behind by a previous shop owner, more like a long workbench that was shoved against one wall. That night I slept on the table after we cleared it off.

In the morning David put Donovan's *Sunshine Superman* album on a record player and stirred up some oatmeal on a hot plate by the front window. The one-room storefront had heat, electricity, and water but the toilet didn't work so they used the one in The Annex, a bar around the corner on Avenue B. Or sometimes they watered the airshaft out the window between buildings. Before any of the three of us had ventured out, someone knocked at the door. It was John from Lincoln asking for me. Cher had seen him that morning and told him where to find me. I hadn't laid eyes on John for eight or nine months, didn't even know he'd left Lincoln. It seems a lot of people besides me had quit the university and left town. John pointed at me and in a mock imperious tone said, "You! Come with me!" I grinned and together we walked the icy sidewalks to some place a few blocks away and found the other guys from Lincoln.

I was glad to see the familiar faces of my old roommate Grady, last seen in Denver, and Joe Knight, not seen since one of my stops in Chicago. Weren't we all the picture of refugees now, from the dreary Great Plains and the institutional grip of the Establishment. I had to explain to my friends why my hair was so short and how it got cut in the New Mexico jail. They weren't settled in anywhere permanent and were crashing here and there, a little desperate themselves. I told them I was at the storefront and brought them over and David and Danny let them crash there for a couple of nights. We weren't reunited for very long, because in a couple of days they left New York and I never saw any of them again. Rather than join them I stayed where I was with David and Danny to wait for Toni's arrival from New Mexico.

A couple days later Cher came over to the storefront, speculating that an apartment on the sixth floor of her building might be vacant. That is, the occupant had vanished, a guy named Lloyd who hadn't been seen in weeks. The last anyone had heard, he'd said something cryptic about going to the Emerald City. Nobody knew what that meant. Our party of four went over to investigate, climbed five flights of stairs and found the top-floor apartment unlocked. It consisted of three rooms laid out in a rectangle. Entry was right next to the bathtub in the kitchen. There was a larger bedroom to the right of the kitchen and a small room to the left. It was clean, nicely furnished and decorated with cool paintings. This Lloyd guy had more money than us, to fix the dumpy place up so much.

We heard a noise from the closet and discovered a guy either sleeping there or hiding from us. He turned out to be a schoolbus-driver friend of Lloyd's named Cuzo who didn't know where Lloyd was either. He told us it was okay with him if we stayed there. After a couple days with no sign of Lloyd we gradually migrated across the street, carted over books and records, and abandoned the storefront.

A guy named Don West came by with his blonde girlfriend Bethany. He carried a polished walking stick and was dressed in a ruffled shirt and a long cape and top hat, like some dandified coun-terpart of the Civil War soldiers. He wanted to heist some of Lloyd's stuff and try to sell it, starting with a three-foot-high plaster statue of a winged cherub that stood on the kitchen floor next to the gas stove. It looked like it belonged over a tombstone. David and I shrugged and trailed behind him into the snowy night while he wandered from junk shop to antique store hoping to get some cash for it. We rational-ized that it was Don ripping off Lloyd, not us, although he was willing to give us a cut of whatever he could get for it. New York was an inter-esting place, where no one minded a guy dressed like a riverboat gambler walking around the busy streets at night with a three-foot cupid statue.

The few shops we went to, Don told us to wait outside. "We can't all three go in or we'll scare them. You guys look pretty shabby, too." Possible buyers might think we were drug addicts, like the junkies in the park who took my glasses when I was asleep. But no one would buy it from him either. Shopkeepers didn't want to risk being arrested on the charge of receiving stolen goods, which too many thieves tried to pass off on them. We brought the statue back to the apartment and

Don left and that was the last we saw of him. We didn't try to sell anything else.

A night or two later a couple of men in suits showed up at the apartment, one claiming he was Lloyd's dad, trying to locate Lloyd.

"What have you done to him?" he wanted to know.

"Nothing. We haven't seen him," David said.

"I followed you in a car the other night, when you were walking around with this thing," he said, pointing to the cupid. The fact he was shadowing us gave me the creeps, a reminder of the Albuquerque cops who had done likewise. How often were any of us followed and unaware of our stalkers?

"That other guy was trying to sell it. It wasn't us," said David. He had a guileless manner that was convincing.

"I don't care about that anyway. This stuff of Lloyd's is all junk to me. I just want to know he's all right."

Again we said we didn't know where Lloyd was, and he seemed to believe us.

"Then what are you people doing here?" he asked. There was an embarrassed pause.

"We're kinda looking after his place until he comes back," I said, inventing a noble motive on the spot.

"Well when he does, let me know," he said, and gave us a phone number. We hadn't been able to lock the door until then, and he got us a key and allowed us to stay there.

As long as we paid the rent, the building manager didn't concern himself with who was actually living there. In a couple of weeks a furniture dealer came by and took all the furniture and the cupid and the paintings that Lloyd was late on payments for. We refurnished his place with a table and assorted wooden chairs we scavenged from the sidewalks. There was always something useful that someone had abandoned on the street. Pretty soon Lloyd's became a crash pad and gathering hub, a revolving door for two or three dozen souls. At any one time a menagerie of people could be found there—someone who knew someone, or came with a friend, or just got invited over by one of us while out on the street.

The ones who kept coming back began to form a cadre of regulars. There were a few Chicagoans who all seemed to know each other already, but none that I remembered from Wells Street. Others were just a subway or ferry ride from middle class neighborhoods where they grew up. As kids they'd been coming over to Greenwich Village to see the beatnik poets and the folk singers and the jazz musicians, and heard it all on the local radio stations as well. I was envious. They had every advantage, to live right where everything cool was happening. Even now they had a lifeline to home and could stop off any time for a meal or to get their laundry done, or get their mail or anything else they needed. They hadn't quit their families like I had, and their families hadn't quit them, like mine did.

I failed to realize then that even the renegade Allen Ginsberg had his beginnings a subway ride from Greenwich Village. Jack Kerouac wasn't hitchhiking through the Mojave Desert when he was eighteen, like I did. All the time when I'd thought I was following a trail blazed by others, I'd only been chasing my own mirage. Now my plan was get my feet under me again. Having a quasi-permanent place on the map to stay put, I didn't see myself getting back on the road any time soon, especially since I was waiting out Toni's release. If it wasn't my apartment, it was as much mine as anyone else's and I wasn't under any pressure to move on.

The smaller room at Lloyd's had an Oriental rug and a little stained-glass fixture that put out a cozy light. Six or eight of us would sit slumped against the walls listening to Indian ragas by Ravi Shankar and burning incense sticks. No way any of this was foot-tapping teenage dance music. It was for meditation.

The new Beatles album *Revolver* had been out for a few months but I hadn't heard it until now. In four years since "I Want to Hold Your Hand" the Beatles had come a long way. The track "Tomorrow Never Knows" had a sitar background and lyrics like "turn off your mind" and "surrender to the void." It would be a mistake to hear it as inducement to take more psychedelics. It was more than that, another mystic communiqué like the *Tao Te Ching*, reminding me to continue looking for the Way, or more specifically, reminding me that there even was a Way to be found.

We also played new record albums like *The Doors* and *Surrealistic Pillow*. The Doors and Jefferson Airplane lacked any dimension. Commercial entertainment like theirs was run by an industry of people out to make money, not expand our consciousness. "Light My Fire" and "White Rabbit" were aimed at a mass market of consumers. They wouldn't change the world or end war and racism.

There was nothing mass market about *The 13th Floor Elevators*, from Austin, Texas. Their reverb guitars, banshee vocals and mystic lyrics were too mind-blowing to be called mass entertainment. They were more uniquely psychedelic than the so-called San Francisco sound, and although they played often in San Francisco they weren't heard on the radio. They were sonic LSD, some kind of electrified echoing *Book of the Dead* for guidance through the bardo. I heard in them the message I'd heard in Allen Ginsberg's "shake hands with a cloud."

I sent my parents my address and they forwarded a letter to me from the Selective Service. Inside could be a death sentence in the form of a notice to report for induction. Instead it was a 1-Y card, a welcome reprieve from 1-A. It meant I was eligible still, but not likely to ever be put in uniform. Only as a last resort. I guessed my New Mexico episode had been too much for the high standards they required to slog through rice paddies planted with land mines. From my point of view, being in the county jail was the luckiest thing that ever happened to me.

CHAPTER 26

A hillbilly tramp from the midwest like myself wasn't polished enough for glitzy Greenwich Village. If the beatnik coffee houses where famous poets and folk singers got their start were still around, I couldn't afford to go in them. I belonged a few blocks east of there, past the subway stop at Astor Place, in the Lower East Side. To me, Greenwich Village with its Chelsea Hotel and NYU was privileged and commercial. It compared to the Lower East Side the way LA compared to San Francisco.

Some nights we bundled up and ventured out in the cold. The Psychedelicatessen on Avenue B resembled the Psychedelic Shop on Haight Street, selling cigarette-rolling papers and hash pipes and Aldous Huxley books. They had a few posters of moiré patterns and a little exhibit that featured a spinning paper disc with a design on it. When you stared at it and looked away, the after-image in your eyes made everything seem to continue whirling for a little while. A man standing nearby said, "Look at it and then look at your hand." He meant that your skin looked like it was shimmering and vibrating. "It does that anyway," said someone, and we all laughed, because we were high and didn't need any prompting by a spinning disc. Everything seemed to emanate a visible dance of molecules on its surface already. Even the snow outside sparkled purple and yellow and green.

Weeks after Toni and I were busted in New Mexico and separated by the authorities, she was free once more and we reunited at Lloyd's. The bummer was that she was living with her parents and had to be home every night. I went up to meet her family, who lived in a large apartment in the upper east side. It was nothing fashionable, just middle-class, but much larger than the tenements I was used to. They were friendly to me, hospitable, didn't put me on the spot and make me nervous. Toni's dad was enormously obese. I had no idea what he did or how they came to be living there. Toni had a younger brother living with them too. So including the weird older brother in New Mexico, there were three siblings of widely separated ages. I didn't know how Toni had come to be in New Mexico when I met her the first time. Being the untalkative sort that I was, I didn't ask all the questions that you normally would to get to know people, about their pasts and their lives. I took everyone as I found them and all that mattered was the present. They didn't cross-examine me either, so I didn't have to explain about stuff like Toni and me and the drunk drivers in Texas, or the Hells Angel in Chicago, or the Diggers in San Francisco, or any of the other people and places we'd seen.

At the end of March, David, Keith, and I rode the subway to Central Park to meet Toni for the Easter Be-In at Sheep Meadow. Though it was a sunny day, the ground was still cold after the spring thaw. On a slight hillside with the wide, still-brownish meadow largely empty behind us, we spread out a blanket at the fringe of the crowd and dropped acid. The Be-In was a toned-down east coast version of the Human Be-In two months earlier in San Francisco, and less struc-tured than the indoor happening I'd gone to in Boulder. There might have been drums somewhere distant, the eternal conga drums of New York parks, but no central stage or activity or celebrity presence. No one was providing entertainment and for anyone who was expecting some, the only attraction was the large milling crowd itself.

We were happy just to be there tripping on all the people who'd come with no ulterior purpose than to be present.

It was impossible to tell who had wandered into the gathering out of curiosity and who belonged to the hippie head culture newly emerging across the country. The outward signs of costume and hair weren't very prominent yet. Keith had dressed for the part as well as anyone—wearing an Indian blanket and a fur Cossack hat and a large bead necklace.

Despite the numbers, throughout the day it felt like a small and peaceful gathering. Some groups sat holding hands in meditation circles, obviously tripping. A mellow place to be on acid, no bad trips here. Most milled around sharing the warm weather and good energy. People freely passed around joints. Some sat on the huge rocks and a few perched in the bare tree limbs. For long stints I stood poised motionless and speechless, morphed into a tall and spindly Masai herder overlooking the amicable masses swirling by me.

It was a Be-In, not a happening, not a concert or rally, neither commercial nor political. There was no pageantry. It wasn't a spectacle. There were no carnival barkers, then or after, to memorialize it with some Woodstock glory. Dig it: a gathering for the purpose of simply being there, more friendly and open than the crowds we were usually part of on the streets. For a few hours, strangers could assemble without eyeing each other suspiciously.

I walked Toni to her parents' door as the afternoon faded, and rode the subway back down to Astor Place. It was hard to tell where I left the concentrated one-day Be-In and re-entered the citywide human be-in that never ended.

As spring arrived, the East Village over past St Marks Place was a land of old Ukrainian women in babushkas sitting on the front steps of their apartment buildings, of concentration camp survivors on park benches feeding the pigeons, of men playing chess on the concrete chess tables in the park. There were Puerto Rican youth gangs to be wary of, that would mug you at night. It was a place of bums routinely passed out on the sidewalk, or asleep, or overdosed or possibly dead. There were so many that you had to give up your instinct to help and learn to just walk past them like the native New Yorkers. In Tompkins Square Park the handball courts were busy and groups of drummers with their tall conga drums saturated the air with a primitive pulse for hours on end. In an area of a few square blocks, the Lower East Side was a panorama of life never glimpsed in Lincoln, Nebraska.

My onetime girlfriend Darlene was back in New York. She wore a floppy broad-brimmed hat and high purple boots with a little chain wrapped around one at the ankle. She lived over on East 8th with some drug dealer guy named Corky who always seemed to be away in San Francisco. The only time I met Corky, he answered the door and Darlene was out. He gave me a free tab of acid to try because he wasn't sure how good it was and was considering buying a large quantity to resell. It was good, but I never saw him again to tell him it was worth buying.

Whenever I went to their building the first flight of indoor stairs was likely to be occupied by a kid maybe twelve or thirteen and sometimes his girlfriend. He'd be holding a paper bag and staring off into glue-sniffing land, not even seeming to notice me. I hadn't heard about sniffing glue until then. Having tried Asthmador and Vicks inhalers, I might have experimented with it, if I hadn't been occupied with grass, hash, DMT, mescaline, and acid. Luckily, I found out in time that glue permanently melts brain cells that you never get back. Eats holes in the Serbian cortex and the antebellum frobotomy, ranking somewhere below drinking Sterno—not even made for the human organism. Eventually it turns you into a dead spider on its back with dried legs sticking up in the air.

Sometimes Toni and I went over to Darlene's together. One night we found Billy Neighbor visiting, the guy in Chicago who I'd turned on to selling the load of crystal. He said he'd made $2,000 from that deal, a fortune. It was almost the price of a new Ford Mustang. I could have lived for a year on that amount, but no way was it enough to make me wish I'd gotten involved in Chicago meth deals.

It was a small world, seemed like, so many people from far flung places showing up in unexpected coincidences the way Darlene from Lincoln and Billy from Chicago did. Or Tim from Chicago being in Denver when I was, Chuck appearing in Albuquerque, and Grady in New York. Now here was Billy with a couple kilos of grass in his suitcase that I guess he was buying from or selling to Corky, who wasn't there.

We were about to roll a joint when someone knocked at the door. Darlene called out who was it and they identified themselves as police. She couldn't exactly tell them to go away. Darlene had what was called a railroad apartment, with a hallway along one side that opened into the different rooms like rail car compartments. I snatched the grass we were about to smoke and walked down the hallway to flush it down the toilet. The two plainclothes came in and one of them hurried to see what I was doing, but by then the evidence was gone.

We all grouped in the front room and had to show our IDs. This was beginning to feel like a rerun of the New Mexico trouble that Toni and I had been in, but they weren't interested in us. These New York cops seemed a lot cooler about the small stuff. They'd seen it all I guess. They were looking for Corky, and even Darlene didn't know where he was. All this time I was thinking about Billy's suitcase with the dope standing over in the corner. Maybe they were just looking for information but I wanted to get out of there in case they were going to search the place. I asked was it okay to leave because Toni had to get back to her parents. There was a curfew in those days as well, and they said we could go.

That little incident was close enough for me. Over the next few weeks I got to thinking about Toni and me. We'd had some adventures. I had brought her from Albuquerque to Chicago, then to San Francisco. Had followed her to Albuquerque again and then to New York. Two arrests for her and a close call with New York detectives. I had a glum outlook on our present situation. If I was twenty-four and she was twenty-one it would be different. I was nineteen now and she was a sixteen-year-old kid living at home. I didn't think I could maintain a subway commuter relationship. She was restored to her family where she belonged and should have been in school instead of hanging out with somebody like me. I hoped she would have a better future but I wasn't able to explain my thoughts that logically. In some manner I told her that it wasn't like it had been in San Francisco and I wasn't going to see her any more. It was awful, and I felt crummy about making her unhappy.

We were gathered in Lloyd's kitchen to light and pass around small chunks of hash or DMT. You put a piece in a pipe with a kitchen faucet filter screen in the bowl so you wouldn't inhale it through the pipe stem, just the smoke. Nathan tried to break off a little piece of white waxy DMT crystal and dropped it by accident. Nathan and Valerie and David and Peggy and Keith and all of us were down on the scuffed and unfinished wood floor picking up specks of food, lint, dirt or anything else that resembled a precious crumb of DMT. It was expensive compared to grass and you only had to smoke a tiny portion. The high was like mild acid and lasted for about twenty minutes.

Another night we were sitting around the kitchen table smoking pot and David brought up a rumor that got started in *The Berkeley Barb*. "They're saying you can get high on dried banana peels," he said. We all laughed about that.

"You think it's true?" asked Keith, toking on a joint and passing it to me. He might've been the youngest person in the whole group. Despite a deep voice and great coarse sideburns that made him seem older, Keith had the enthusiasm and innocence of a kid. He lived in Queens where he grew up, and spent as many nights crashing on our floor as he did at home.

"That can't be true," said Valerie, a Staten Island native and David's girlfriend of the moment. She had long light brown hair and a nervous habit of stuffing handfuls of it up to her mouth.

"Like Donovan's song about the "eee-lec-tric-al banana," I said, pronouncing the word the way he did in his song, and passing the joint to Nathan, a part-Hawaiian kid from Grand Rapids, Michigan.

"Yeah but we have to try it," said Nathan's girlfriend Ann. She was skinny and wore her hair in a long thick braid most of the time. She had kind of a Katy Jurado face with smoldering eyes and a pouting mouth.

'We have to,' said Marty. He was a Chicagoan, a freckled runty guy who would get high with us and then stare into a mirror saying, "God I can't believe how wasted I look. Look at me. I'm so stoned. God."

For three days we carefully scraped the inner pulp from banana skins until we had a sizable lump. We baked it for a while and when it was dry and somewhat crumbly Nathan laughingly did the honors of rolling it. We usually used Zig-Zag or JOB papers that we bought at Gem Spa or the Psychedelicatessen.

"So here we go," announced Nathan, lighting up the first joint.

"I think I'm getting a buzz," said David, after he took his puff on it. Marty laughed. "Really?"

I took a skeptical electrical toke and held in the smoke.

"Oh man. It's working," Ann said. We wanted to believe it was true, but nobody really did.

"Hand me those matches," said Keith. The banana peel joint kept going out.

"I'm dizzy from holding my breath," Valerie said.

It was all a hoax, a ruse to get the police and government stirred up and on a wild chase in their zeal to crack down on anything that the underground was doing. At some point Marty ventured that we should smoke some real dope. He never contributed any grass of his own though, but was always mooching off of others. "Give me a mirror. God, I look so wasted! I can't believe how stoned I look."

Weeks later, as a group of us sat around the kitchen, a couple guys knocked at the door and someone let them in. Most of us paid them no mind, since people were coming and going all the time. It was only after a few moments that David said, "It's Lloyd!" He was the only one who'd ever actually met Lloyd before he disappeared.

We all gaped at a bearded guy in a fedora and tweed sports coat, slightly older than us, heavyset like his dad.

"Lloyd?"

Lloyd looked around and beamed. "This is great," he said. He seemed pleased that his apartment was occupied by a dozen or so strangers. Nor did he seem to mind that all his furniture had been reclaimed. He was living somewhere else, I gathered, and wasn't ready to move back in.

CHAPTER 27

S treet Freak Carol walked in the door and came over next to me at the cash register.

"Kiss me," she said. She squeezed her eyes shut and puckered her lips, waiting.

"No thanks," I said with an embarrassed chuckle, and she opened her eyes. She did this a couple times a week, I supposed to the other guys who worked there too. I wasn't real sure kissing would be a hygienic thing to do.

She could have been Toni's age, with a wide face and frizzy blondish hair emanating out to her shoulders. She could handle herself and I liked her streetwise confidence. She was a for-real "Slum Goddess of the Lower East Side," like The Fugs sang about.

A parade of girls passed through the Underground Uplift Unlimited every day, hanging out, listening to the records, not buying anything. Some were regulars in the neighborhood, others exploring. For a nineteen-year-old like me they were quite a diversion. It was far better than slaving at the Rawlins plant in Chicago. A lot of them rode the subway in from home, but I don't think Carol lived anywhere permanent, therefore the nickname Street Freak. I didn't mind her hanging around. I guess I did kiss her a couple times, just to surprise us both.

. . .

St Marks Place (or maybe St. Mark's Place, with all its punctuations) was the main gateway to the East Village, as much a tourist destination as Greenwich Village, but sketchier. People came to get a taste of the bohemian experience. It already had a long history, and another layer of cultural sediment was sifting down to supersede the beatniks. In 1967 St Marks Place was the Manhattan version of Haight Street in San Francisco. Without realizing it, we were joining others of our kind, the great youth surge of the Sixties flocking to urban centers of counterculture, some to seek thrills, some teenage independence.

Between Second and Third Avenues, at 28 St Marks Place, Underground Uplift Unlimited was the most touristy shop on the street. The main feature of the Uplift's display window was a WWII aerial bomb casing, painted bright yellow and hanging at a nose-down angle as if in a dive. Forget about the bald eagle and the Statue of Liberty. Bombs and dollars were America's true symbols. The sign over the entrance was a black-and-white hand-painted cartoon of the eye-in-a-triangle on the back of a dollar bill, with lines radiating from the triangle as if to represent an aura of holy light. The opposite of a Peace Eye.

I had all the keys to the front door, the upper deadbolt, and the police lock if I opened in the morning, or if I closed at night. The store was a couple of steps down from the sidewalk, with a small plaza area in front of it, a quiet eddy where street people liked to hang out. Until New York I hadn't seen buildings like that, the kind where the first floor was submerged part way below street level so that from inside you saw a parade of legs and feet passing the window.

The Uplift sold round metal slogan buttons, the election-campaign kind with pins on the back for attaching to your clothes, sort of a personal bumper sticker in the age before anyone had tattoos. Some had contemporary slogans like "Make Love, Not War," "Keep The Faith Baby," and "Burn Baby Burn." There were dozens of buttons in all color combinations and fonts. The store owners kept adding new ones to broaden their inventory: "Legalize Marijuana," "Flower Power," "Nirvana Now," "Don't Trust Anyone Over 30." The silly ones sold as often as the others: "Marcel Proust is a Yenta," "Dracula Sucks." I never wore them myself, and I noticed the owners didn't either. I generally avoided being labelled, but I would have worn a peace-symbol button if I was ever at a special occasion like a peace march, which in New York I never was.

For button purchases the Uplift used small white coin envelopes printed with the eye-in-the-triangle logo on the front. They came in two sizes that just happened to be perfect for a nickel of grass in the small ones and a one-ounce lid in the bigger ones.

Along with buttons, the Uplift sold posters, mostly psychedelic art or counterculture themes. We had posters on all the walls and the ceiling, such as "Better Living Through Chemistry" and Rick Griffin's colorful drawing of a hookah and liquid lettering of "A puff of kief in the morning makes a man as strong as a hundred camels in the courtyard."

Nathan and David were first to get jobs at Underground Uplift Unlimited. They said the owners were gay, but treated everyone properly and didn't act weird around them. As soon as he had money, Nathan came back to the apartment one day with a sitar, inspired by Ravi Shankar and George Harrison. It didn't strike me as one of the first things I'd do if I suddenly had cash. Both my friends managed to get themselves fired pretty quick, quite an achievement considering there wasn't anything challenging about the work. Maybe they had been too stoned on the job and botched it. I walked over and applied for work, careful not to mention that I knew either David or Nathan. They hired me and another guy. I didn't have to cut my hair, not that my hair was fully restored from the shearing in New Mexico. I was working on it though. The other guy didn't show much energy on the job and it wasn't long before he was let go because as the owner put it, "He's a brown rice man." I wasn't sure what that made me.

I wrote a letter:

I'm taking home $64 a week from my job, which is a fairly simple and undemanding one, and a lot of fun besides. I tend one of the little shops in the Village—only not the popular touristy, commercial, superficial part of the Village but down on the Lower East Side.... I really like it here...it's all right smack in the middle of the freakiest spot in the country next to Haight-Ashbury...

My parents probably weren't encouraged to read I was living in a place described as the freakiest, but my intent was to announce that I was off the road and stabilized in one place, and not dead yet.

I could buy food and clothes that I'd gone without for the past two years, and Ballantine Ale by the quart. In a better life I would be finishing my second year of college. Those were the three choices I saw laid before me: college, counterculture, or combat—and I absolutely positively wasn't going to carry a rifle.

The Uplift's owner didn't look like a radical underground type at all. More like a kid in a plain white T-shirt who delivered newspapers or mowed lawns. He was smaller than me, wiry, with a collegiate haircut, boyish features and blue eyes with constricted pupils. We knew him as Randy Wicker. He was prominent in gay rights activism and the Mattachine Society, a gay advocacy group, and to some he became a legend, but all that activity was kept separated from the store.[1] While he exuded energy and intensity, his partner Peter Ogren was more easy going. He had short-cropped blond hair that gave him a sort of Ivy League, Roman aristocrat look. He talked in a higher voice with a mild singsong lilt like some gays did, but without a lisp.

Randy and Peter didn't hire women during the time I was there. I wondered if it was an unspoken policy. Most of us who worked there were straight. Maybe everybody was, though I had suspicions about a couple of guys. Having met Allen Ginsberg and Peter Orlovsky, and having heard my friend Steve Abbott's confession, I wanted to co-exist, live and let live, but I had no desire to find out more details. Gay rights, women's liberation, and disability rights were still over the horizon. For most people, civil rights and antiwar causes were on our minds.

I tried to ignore my anxiety over the whole idea of homosexuals, but to a kid who'd practically walked across Nebraska—definitely not a gay thing to do—they were sort of frightening. It was a primal aversion, not a conscious prejudice. I guessed if you grew up in New York you got used to them. I was pretty sure that all the labels of the past— flit, homo, fag, fruit, queer—were not too kind. You had to unlearn the disrespectful names in common usage for all the different kinds of Puerto Ricans, Italians, Poles, blacks, and straights. And I still didn't like being called a hippie.

"Gimme a quarter." Humphrey made a daily appearance in the store to get a handout. "We was black buffaloes." He was a small black man with missing teeth and reddened eyes, a tweed fedora and a black trench coat, expounding in a gravelly voice about his service in the WWII Black Buffalo 92nd Infantry.

"Hiya Humphrey." He was predictable. Our instructions were to give him a quarter out of the till and leave a chit for it. I opened the register as soon as he shambled in. No doubt he had trained a legion of store clerks and I had to admire his strategy of making regular rounds like the milkman.

"1945 black buffaloes," he mumbled some more. I thought of the Blackstone Rangers.

"Here you go, Humphrey." He ignored my attempts at other topics and I tuned out his recitation of regiment, division, battalion. I respected that his war had at least been to some humanitarian purpose, unlike the current one. I could even see myself serving back then.

That spring I got my fourth and final draft card in the mail. After being 2-S, 1-A, and 1-Y, I had achieved the ultimate rank of 4-F, not qualified for military service. To me it was like making Eagle Scout. The Vietnam albatross I had been carrying for a year and a half was finally lifted. Not being a marked man took getting used to.

. . .

People came in with merchandise to sell to us at wholesale, or leave on commission. In no time Underground Uplift's stock expanded to include day-glo paint, black lights, strobe lights, "trip glasses" made of colored glass crystals that we glued into plastic eyeglass frames, Zodiac pendants, water pipes, pipe screens, and diffraction discs.

Randy had a nice sound system in the store for music at all times, to provide atmosphere and keep customers in the store listening. Sometimes he told us to buy a record with money from the till, knowing we'd pick out the newest music that people wanted to hear. Conveniently, there was a record store a few doors down the street. My first choice was *The 13th Floor Elevators.* Then as they were released, the Grateful Dead's first album in March, Jimi Hendrix's *Are You Experienced* in May, the Sgt. Pepper album in June, and later that summer, *Vanilla Fudge.* We were the cutting-edge DJs on the block.

We turned the Uplift into a perpetual Acid Test. Free admission, no cover charge, no minimum. So much for a mellow, laid-back Lower East Side antidote to the glitzy Greenwich Village. The place was jammed with tourists on weekend nights, vibrating with loud music, flashing lights, day-glo everywhere, incense burning, and the ka-ching of the cash register. It was more psychedelic than the Psychedelicatessen. The only things lacking were swirling color projections, a live band, and free acid.

A mannish chick about thirty in an olive drab army jacket and crushed Breton cap came in on a slow afternoon. While I finished with a customer she looked at our table of radical publications that included *East Village Other, San Francisco Oracle,* and *The Realist.*

When we were alone she handed me her product sample, a few pages run off on a mimeograph and stapled together. "Do you want to carry my newsletter?" It was titled *SCUM Manifesto,* a publication of the Society for Cutting Up Men.

"I gotta call the owner," I told her. Below the title, I read her name, Valerie Solanas.

"It's fifty cents wholesale. Women get charged a dollar and men two dollars," Valerie said. She seemed pretty friendly to me, and I didn't get any hostile vibes from her like she was ready to cut me up. All the same, I preferred Street Freak Carol and her "Kiss me."

Over the phone Randy told me to buy a dozen copies. I put them out on the table with the reading material. I never read more than a few paragraphs, but I recognized her name and picture about a year later when she was in the news for shooting Andy Warhol.

I didn't do much reading then, especially anything political. The long-term effect of acid made words inadequate, and long written arguments tiresome. Sometimes I skimmed local stories in the *East Village Other*, and studied the crazy artwork in the *Oracle*. I didn't read the *Realist*, except to glance at the May issue. It was a best-seller for its centerpiece drawing of the Disneyland Memorial Orgy of cartoon characters in a melee of debauchery, everyone from Snow White to Goofy.

Every few weeks a guy with long curly hair and ragged beard came in and spent his time browsing through the radical material on the newspaper table. He was much older and we never spoke. He was very quiet, almost deferential it seemed. The first time we met he showed me a handful of assorted papers he wanted to take.

"Randy said I could have these." He said his name was Tuli Kupferberg and to call Randy Wicker. Randy affirmed that Tuli could take any papers he wanted any time without paying. I didn't know Tuli was a friend of Allen Ginsberg, and also a famous poet, although not a household name like Ginsberg. I sort of knew that he was one of The Fugs, but didn't realize he had helped start the Peace Eye Bookstore with Ed Sanders. Even if I had, I felt intimidated by the stature of all those seasoned beatniks. Plus I was drifting away from poetry after the direct, nonverbal effects of acid. I lost interest in words and wasn't looking to connect with poets any more.

. . .

Lloyd decided he wanted to move back into his apartment, so we all had to find other places. By May I had my own apartment on East 9th Street, across the street from Lloyd's and close to the building where David and Danny had occupied their storefront. Instead of being up five flights of stairs, I had the luxury of being on the second floor. Like Lloyd's, the three cockroach-colonized rooms had a bathtub in the kitchen and a steel bar to wedge the door against break-ins. The toilet was the first of its kind I'd never seen. Its water tank was mounted high up on the wall and had a chain to pull down on to flush it. I put gates in the soot-covered windows to keep out junkies sneaking in from the fire escape. When I was away I left the radio on as an extra caution, so that to a prowler it sounded like someone was home.

Now that I had an income these were affluent times. Just about every night friends gathered on the floor in the living room area with me. A lot of the former crowd from Lloyd's were there, including Keith, who donated a stereo system. I kept grass out in a wooden bowl for anyone to roll a joint, and a kitchen strainer to sift out the stems and most of the seeds. The seeds that got through the strainer popped when they got hot, making sort of a stoner's exploding cigar. Lit by red and green light bulbs in the ceiling fixture, we spaced out and hardly moved, passing around joints. We burned incense and listened to The Blues Project *Projections* album and other records, or WBAI radio. The languid evenings were the opposite of the frenzied atmosphere at the Uplift.

When it grew late some people left and the rest of us fell asleep where we were for the night. Despite my shyness, sometimes one of the girls who haunted the Underground Uplift followed me home after I locked up at closing time, and I might have to usher my other visitors out. After all, the news from San Francisco was that it was the Summer of Love. On one occasion four girls hovered near as I locked up the store, all day-trippers who commuted from home by subway. I felt like they were waiting to pounce on me. Street Freak Carol happened to be drifting by on the sidewalk, a genuine Slum Goddess, and to escape the mob I swept her along home with me.

· · ·

We walked down towards Houston Street one night to buy a few ounces of grass, me and a friend, guided by a guy in his older twenties we knew. He said the people there were paranoid about strangers and he'd have to go in alone. We pooled our money and waited outside for him. He came back out with a paper grocery bag containing large cans with vegetable and fruit labels that were much too light. Back at my place we opened one and it was the real deal—marijuana in a can. Some serious people ran an operation like that.

Another night Keith and I were in my kitchen with a guy I didn't know too well who wanted to buy more grass than I had on hand. Keith said he knew where he could get some. I vouched that he was trustworthy and the guy gave him forty dollars and Keith went out alone. After about thirty minutes he was back, empty-handed.

The first thing the guy said was, "Where's the grass?"

"I got robbed," Keith said.

"Robbed! What about my forty dollars?"

"I was just a few blocks away and got mugged on the sidewalk." I could see Keith was upset about it, that he wasn't acting.

"He's telling the truth," I told the guy. Keith didn't rip people off. Had he done that he wouldn't have come back to us with a made-up story.

The guy was disgusted about losing his forty dollars, gone for good. "Why didn't you put the money in your shoe?"

I felt lousy for both of them, but all I could do was reassure him that Keith was not a cheat. Just the opposite, he was always doing things to help, as he had tried to do this time.

I was only mugged once. Walking home at night on East 9th, I was surrounded by teenage Puerto Ricans, about four of them, and one put a knife up to my throat. They walked me through a tenement door and into the back of the hallway where they could search me for money without being seen. I didn't have a wallet, and no money, so they said I could go. I walked down the hallway with a prickly sensation at my back, wondering all the while if they were going to knife me. It would have made no sense, since they wanted money, not blood, but I was too inexperienced to know. From then on, whenever

I had money I carried it in my shoe or my sock, but I was never waylaid again. I also practiced keeping a better eye on my surroundings. You had to stay watchful.

On June 1st, some of us went to a free Grateful Dead concert at the Tompkins Square Park bandshell, two blocks from my place on East 9th. Their debut album had come out only two months before and I'd bought it to play in the Uplift. They didn't have any hit singles and most people outside of the San Francisco area hadn't heard of them yet. A couple weeks later they played at the Monterey Pop Festival.

A poetry magazine that had my writing in it came in the mail from Cleveland, but it wasn't new work. Carl Woidek's *Sum* wasn't any newer than my last visit to Cleveland, just slow to catch up to me.[2] Then a letter came from Walter Lowenfels.[3] I vaguely thought I'd heard that name somewhere. He asked to use a poem of mine that I had read at The Gate nearly a year before, for an anthology he was putting together to be published by Doubleday. He might have seen it in d. a. levy's *Poets at the Gate*. He included a contract for me to sign and return—my permission in exchange for five dollars and two copies of the book when it came out. I agreed. So would Tuli Kupferberg and Ed Sanders, I would find out, and Allen Ginsberg and many other poets already famous or soon to be.

CHAPTER 28

W alking to the Uplift took me past the enduring landmark at the corner of Second Avenue, Gem Spa, a walk-up soda fountain and news stand. I went there for chocolate egg creams, the *Village Voice*, wheat straw rolling papers, and Gauloises cigarettes in the blue package. The Underground Uplift Unlimited was only a few doors up the block.

On my way to the Uplift I spotted Emmett Grogan in front of Gem Spa. It was probably six months since I'd seen him. In the midst of New York's cramped and claustrophobic streets it was refreshing to meet someone I associated with San Francisco. We spoke for a few moments before I continued on to the store. Some weeks later the other Digger that Toni and I used to hang out with more often, Billy Murcott, came into the Uplift. At the time I didn't know that both he and Emmett were originally from New York. Billy had some acid to sell and I knew it would be good stuff and not a ripoff. It was a good price so I gave him enough for ten tabs and an Underground Uplift envelope to take into the bathroom to put them into. It turned out to be good acid and I turned a few people on with some of it. Coming from Billy, it could've been Owsley acid.

I never tried to work at the Underground Uplift on acid though because of the tripped-out magic it put me in. I'd get lost counting out ten "Make Love, Not War" buttons. It would have been impossible to keep track of prices or money. I wouldn't smoke pot before going to work, because it left me too hypnotized to function. It also increased my paranoia. I couldn't even walk down the street on pot. But on rare times when I could get it, mescaline was a happy compromise between acid and grass.

On mescaline I was serene, in control and upbeat. People had that shimmering aura, the past and future disappeared, and I could be present in the moment. It helped me feel connected with customers or anyone else who came into the store. Two straight-looking women who were obvious tourists bought a few buttons and a poster and as I rang them up I noticed one button was "Keep the Faith, Baby!" After I made change and put their purchases in a bag I had the uncharacteristic sense to remind them, "Keep the faith now." They smiled and knew that I wasn't being sarcastic. It was as if to say, "Y'all come back now."

One explanation for the store's continuous traffic was across the street, a large building called The Dom. Soon it was renamed The Balloon Farm, presenting Andy Warhol's Exploding Plastic Inevitable. On opening night a flatbed truck parked in front of it, carrying two giant search lights. From the store I watched their beams sweeping the sky. Later in the year demolition chutes spilled debris from upper windows into dump trucks and the place was renovated into the Electric Circus, a light show and glitzy music club with curving walls inside. I went in once as a friend's guest for a few minutes and watched him work. His job was manipulating the food coloring and oils on the overhead transparency projectors that created part of the ambient light show. I never saw any of the live performances there, just a few musicians who came into the Uplift when I happened to be working the register. Barry Melton, from Country Joe and the Fish. One of the Chambers Brothers, the guys with the epic song "Time Has Come Today." He was wearing a black suit and white shirt, but for a necktie he had some thick strands of red and yellow yarn.

From time to time Lincoln people happened in, friends and

acquaintances I hadn't seen in a year or longer. My Latvian high school friend Dace Grots. Professor of English Audrey Christofferson. Carl Davidson of SDS, whose focus on rhetoric and political theory was like my former passion for poetic words. Both forms of verbal chaos seemed so futile to me now. I invited him to my apartment after work. If he hadn't turned me down I would have turned him on.

My old friend Steve Abbott wandered in too. He asked me to come along to see Kenneth Anger's *Scorpio Rising*, already a few years old. I didn't know anything about it, only that it was sort of an underground sensation about motorcycles. I thought it might be a relative of *The Wild Angels*, the movie that the Hells Angel was publicizing when Toni and I were in Chicago. It wasn't. It had a home movie quality featuring Nazi flags and gay bikers in black leather that left me disappointed. Still, I appreciated that it wasn't a Lincoln, Nebraska sort of film. The short movie was paired in a double-feature with *Marat/Sade*. Even more bored, I fell asleep. Neither movie depicted the kind of revolution I had thought of back when I'd seen the graffiti REVOLUTION '66. Steve and I had dinner somewhere and that was the last time I saw him. Neither of us knew he'd be married, and then widowered, and later in the Seventies make history of a sort in San Francisco, among other things editing *Poetry Flash*.

What with Steve Abbott, Carl Davidson, and the other Lincoln people, it was as though all roads led to the Underground Uplift Unlimited. The Underground Uplift was also a mail order business. The "catalog" was a mimeograph list of the slogans, with no images to go by. Price was the same as in the store, twenty-five cents each or five for a dollar, and progressively less as quantity increased. Orders came in from individuals and from small stores everywhere around the country. Some mornings I worked at the office in Randy and Peter's large apartment, opened the mail, sorted out the checks and money, typed mailing labels for the shipments.

I was surprised to open an order for five buttons from Steve

Wilson, whose painting Darlene had hung in my attic room. It was the final irony to find myself sending souvenirs to his mother's address in Lincoln, so he could be hip in Nebraska. The so-called outlaw motorcyclist, six years older than me, was like the teenyboppers who came on the subway to purchase groovy paraphernalia to wear to high school.

At first we filled all the mail orders in between handling customers in the store. It got to be too much for one person and Randy rented the apartment directly upstairs. He stocked the new mail room with tables and boxes of buttons and all the mailing supplies, and installed an intercom to the shop below. We also had mailing tubes for posters, assorted boxes for trip glasses and necklaces. Two of us, sometimes three, alternated between packaging orders upstairs and working the register downstairs.

Abbie Hoffman and his wife lived in the apartment across the hall from the mail room. I took no interest in Abbie and his self-proclaimed Youth International Party, which consisted of about four people calling themselves Yippies. He was already over thirty and to me he personified the mantra "Don't Trust Anyone Over 30." More than anything else he seemed to concentrate on attracting attention and publicity for himself, the opposite of the Diggers' Emmett Grogan, who avoided publicity.

It wasn't the Diggers, but someone imitating the Diggers, maybe Abbie Hoffman, who arranged a free food handout on St Marks that was announced in the *East Village Other* or some place. One morning a box truck rolled up St Marks and stopped a few doors past the Underground Uplift. Early in the day business was slow enough that I could step into the doorway and witness the giveaway. From the back of the truck some guys passed out yogurt and bagels to the reaching crowd. People in front didn't move away fast enough so the guys in the truck tossed some to people just beyond reach. Then they aimed even farther back and people giggled excitedly when a yogurt broke open and it got on their hands. The guys in the truck threw them overhand, harder and farther, and several more people got splattered with yogurt bombs. They were not laughing. Maybe to Abbie or someone else it was street theater. I went back into the store thinking it was a mean way to treat people who hoped for something to eat. Nothing at all like the Diggers.

Autumn's chill spread across the East River and filtered through the high-rise projects on Avenue D to creep along the grim and perilous tenement avenues of the Lower East Side. I was walking Robin to the subway at Astor Place after she'd spent the night in my apartment—I mean spent the night along with a few other people, not specifically with me personally. It was the gloomy kind of day when even the ubiquitous conga drummers weren't in Tompkins Square Park as we hurried through. Our route took us through stone and brick valleys of garbage cans and wrought-iron tree fences, metal sidewalk delivery doors open to shop cellars, graffiti on walls, streetlight poles plastered with announcements, destitute men passed out curbside, leaves and trash blowing in small eddies.

We threaded the familiar territory on St Marks, where from working at the Uplift I knew most of the street regulars by sight or even by name, and encountered Bill on the sidewalk. It seemed he was always on the block somewhere, a leftover beatnik panhandler old enough to be my father. More acquaintance than friend of mine, Bill wore a warm pea-coat and was hefty and well-nourished. He wasn't one of the really hopeless men like Humphrey. He didn't stake out a regular spot or chant a spare-change mantra.

Robin and I passed near and Bill interrupted his conversation with another man to ask for spare change. His offhand tone wasn't beseeching like most of the panhandlers. Bill knew me by sight and didn't actually expect a handout from a kid like me. He routinely asked almost as a way of saying hello. He would've been startled to get anything. Most times I automatically refused people asking for money or I'd be broke within a few blocks. But this time I was moved by inspiration, as if guided. I bent and scooped up a few of the magnificent red, orange and yellow leaves scattering the sidewalk and without a word passed them into his accepting hand.

I was nearly as surprised as he was and in that instant we both smiled and he thanked me in earnest. Bill's friend beamed and Robin too, and as we walked on to Astor Place she said, "You did a good thing." We were every one of us seekers in that late part of the decade, a time of saints and searchers. It's what had brought us there, Bill included, the kind of zen understanding all of us looked for, the kind you couldn't summon at will or buy in a head shop. It seemed like spontaneous street theater, a moment of perfect awareness, a sidewalk satori that all four of us experienced together.

Darlene had gone out to San Francisco and now she was back from the Summer of Love with a friend, Bethany. I recognized her from the first days at Lloyd's apartment as the blonde who'd been with Don West when he tried to sell the cupid statue. Bethany was from Portland and had Polish ancestry and sanpaku eyes. She and Darlene stayed at my place. Darlene soon moved in with Amen, who we knew from the summer before at the Kew Gardens apartment. The blonde stayed. She was sturdy and industrious, got a job right away. She started cooking meals and chased away all the stray girls and my other friends who crashed there. She knew a good thing when she saw it: a guy with a job and a place to live. Together we got a little table-sized Christmas tree. We didn't live happily ever after but for a while my life turned into a regular domestic scene.

I was behind the counter looking through the *East Village Other* when Abbie burst into the store. The stairway door to his apartment was side-by-side with the Uplift's door and I'd seen him coming and going all the time, but he never stopped in to be friendly or get to know us.

This time he entered with no "Hi, how ya doing?" Instead, "Did that shipment of buttons come in for me yet? Abbie Hoffman?"

"What shipment?" I asked. I hadn't been told to expect anything special. The Vanilla Fudge record ended and I stepped over to the turntable and flipped through our albums, extracting *Are You Experienced* to play next.

"Randy ordered them for me." He meant the owner, Randy Wicker. "They're for the Democratic convention. We're all going to Chicago in August." That was still three or four months away, and politics bored me as much as ever.

"Well, there's no..." I paused to put Jimi Hendrix on the spindle and dropped the needle down. "...there's no package for you here." I would have noticed anything in the area behind the glass counters and cash register. "Why? What's going on at the convention?"

"We're organizing a big protest demonstration there."

I smelled another one of his Yippie stunts coming. Abbie seemed driven to call attention to himself. His previous achievements had been about having his picture in the paper more than changing anything: throwing fake money in the Stock Exchange and creating a sideshow to levitate the Pentagon during the 1967 march in Washington. A few months earlier I'd listened to the YIP-In at Grand Central Station over WBAI as it turned into a riot, witnesses phoning in to describe police beating participants, reporters, and bystanders alike.

"Listen," I said, glancing towards a couple of teenyboppers back among the black lights and day-glo posters, "you don't want people going to Chicago." It was wrong to incite crowds of kids to walk into the certainty of police brutality, head bashings, and broken bones. If he wanted to go himself, fine. I wasn't about to rally to his cause any more than I followed any other self-proclaimed leader.

"Why not?" He had a surprised expression as if just tuning in that I existed.

"The cops are bad there, man. I mean really bad. They'll beat everybody up." I didn't explain about my four arrests just for being on the sidewalk on Wells Street. That was enough exposure to Chicago police methods for me to know they weren't going to tolerate crowds of anti-war demonstrators.

While Jimi's yowling guitar filled the store with "Purple Haze," Abbie looked at me with his mouth hanging open. I could see the gears turning. Chicago was another golden opportunity to get his name in the national headlines and a know-nothing twenty-year-old peon like me wasn't gonna ruin it for him.

"Tell Randy to call me when they come in," he said, and left.

My gaze wandered back down to the *East Village Other*. I'd be sure to make Abbie's concern a top priority.

"Peace," I said to no one.

PART V

SAN FRANCISCO

CHAPTER 29

Iwasn't willing to spend another summer in the city. At least, not that city. Bethany and I flew to San Francisco, where I had hopes of re-entering the laid back atmosphere I'd left a year and a half before. Darlene and Keith helped carry our luggage to the airport and then walked us to our boarding gate. It was the last time I saw either of them.

At first San Francisco did seem a better place. I wrote of my relief to be out of New York: "In the heart of Haight Ashbury, friendlier people... tons of freaks all over the place... sky and the sea and the green life in Golden Gate Park just two blocks away..."

We rented an apartment on Cole Street with a bay window and a bed that pulled down out of a closet in the main room. The biggest inconvenience was that in New York an eighteen-year-old could buy liquor. Even in Cleveland an eighteen-year-old could sit in Adele's Bar and drink beer. In San Francisco you had to be twenty-one to buy anything. Over the summer I risked going into liquor stores anyway.

Exactly as I'd forewarned Abbie Hoffman, the cops in Chicago ran amok and turned the Democratic convention into a mass head-bashing of demonstrators, making August another infamous 1968 milestone. Being one of the Chicago Seven must have been a total success for Abbie. The publicity couldn't fail to flatter his ego more than ever.

I took the written Postal Service exam in September when I turned twenty-one. Right away they hired me to sort mail at Rincon Annex, the big three-story post office in the rundown waterfront area. The San Francisco Postmaster's name was Lim P. Lee. We called him Limpy Lee. I opted to work the swing shift because it paid more and I didn't like getting up in the morning. It didn't matter that by now my hair had been growing for a year and a half. All manner of longhairs and hippies worked there. I was optimistic. In a letter I wrote:

> "Monday I start working for the SF Post Office which is a great hippie employer of this town. I sort mail at night till 2:00 AM for $3.25 an hour. I'll be getting over $200 every other week—nothin' like working for the government! I might even do it for 20 years. A groove huh?"

It was more money than I'd ever made before. Working for the federal government would be my patriotic alternative to military servitude. Bethany found work too, a secretarial job at Fox Plaza on Market Street for a match-making service that had ads on late-night TV.

I ventured over to Haight Street to buy the new *ZAP Comix* that was sold under-the-counter, with R. Crumb's raunchy drawings. After the first issue, *ZAP* added work by other artists, including Lincoln's own S. Clay Wilson. As with his Underground Uplift order from the year before, Wilson continued to cross my path at random. We had some paranormal connection that only a gypsy with Tarot cards could explain.

R. Crumb had variety in his comix, such as Mr. Natural and Fritz the Cat, but Wilson never wavered from the vulgar. His smutty stories featured bikers and pirates, and characters like the Checkered Demon and Star-Eyed Stella. His drawings were more detailed and convoluted than the paintings I'd seen in Lincoln. Like a Wilson trademark, sometimes a sign for Tree Frog Beer appeared in the backgrounds of his cartoons.

I still pictured Wilson as a guy six years older than me and living at home with his mother. The characters in his comix didn't live with their mothers. For that reason, I couldn't summon up much admiration when he became a counterculture icon of sorts. In truth, I envied his seemingly normal origins and supportive home. Years later I grew to realize that Wilson and most of the decade's notable radicals, including those I had met, had had untroubled childhoods compared to mine. It wasn't dysfunctional families, but secure and loving environments that had enabled them to become successful rebels.

I began regarding the swarms of street people on Haight Street with a critical eye. The stragglers left over from the Summer of Love were a movement no longer. Instead of protesting the war or demanding justice and civil rights for all, they seemed too superficial to be a counterculture any more. I saw them as hedonist consumers masquerading as bohemians and perpetuating middle-class establishment habits, spending allowances from home on dope and concerts. When they got older they'd be the ones to cop out, saying, "It was just a phase I went through." They'd aspire to shiny cars, tidy lawns, decorated living rooms, and all the trappings of bourgeois achievement.

The popular image of free love, dope, and musical entertainment was really no different from the straight world's own notion of what constitutes liberty and the pursuit of happiness. It was a consumer-oriented, commercial yin-yang system of hippies and straights. Both ways of life were rooted in material avarice and sensory experience, in primate urges where inner life held no allure.

The Sixties had cruised along without fanfare, and suddenly people realized that the decade was a Thing, to be manifested in bell-bottom pants and Peter Max advertising. Now that acid was illegal, a New York journalist wrote a best-seller about Ken Kesey's acid tests. It was a bring-down to see everything the underculture stood for being exploited, already turning into a for-profit spectacle, a caricature of itself. Tiny Tim and his ukulele went on television. There had to be more to revolution than watching him sing "Tiptoe Through the Tulips."

Not only was I anti-establishment, I was getting to be anti-counterculture. Our generation's idealist values, instead of becoming mainstream, were being co-opted. *ZAP Comix* was an example. What did smutty comic books have to do with transcending America's consumer mentality and finding enlightenment? So much for the Age of Aquarius. The pervasive rhetoric about freedom faded away. My hopes that all the dropouts and poets would change this world for the better evaporated a little more every week.

Early in December a Cleveland acquaintance now living in San Francisco phoned to tell me that d. a. levy was dead, having shot himself at age twenty-six. The news was more personal and dispiriting than the King and Kennedy murders earlier in the year. Levy had encouraged me more than I deserved, taking me to poetry readings, printing my work, bringing me to the Asphodel Bookstore. A lot of people in the poetry world were going to miss his influence and energy.[1] I was disappointed in myself for not having kept in better contact. I hadn't been to Cleveland in two years and wasn't writing any more. I had tumbled further away from connections with people who were as meaningful to me as levy—people like Steve Abbott, Joe Knight, Grady, Toni. It was a reprise of my schoolboy life, abandoning friends forever.

As the new year advanced, I turned into a recluse with a bad case of agoraphobia, sneaking out only long enough to buy beer, wine, and liquor to dilute my anxiety. I dreaded going to work. Sorting mail became unbearably monotonous. After ten months of staring at ZIP codes and pigeon holes, I was so bored that no amount of money could appease me and I quit. "I might even do it for 20 years," I had bantered.

I might have been afflicted with one of those disorders they didn't have a name for yet. Bethany accused me of being down. She said, "You're so down." I had a dark outlook on the world, and I didn't much disagree. There wasn't anything to be positive about. I felt isolated even from her. I watched her participate in the world as always, while I grew remote. I was failing to measure up to a wanton hippie existence. I grew discouraged with life. I couldn't go through the motions of domesticity and social engagement. When my attitude didn't improve, she moved to an apartment on Fell Street across from the Panhandle where the Diggers used to bring afternoon stew. I collected unemployment and lived on my savings for a while.

After a year in California, and about the time the first astronaut walked on the moon, two copies of the Walter Lowenfels poetry anthology from Doubleday arrived,[2] and the contractual check for five dollars. The clothbound volume, typeset on book paper, was a serious upgrade from side-stapled mimeo revolution pamphlets. It cost a lot more than fifty cents, and you knew they printed more than a hundred copies. What surprised me most when I saw it in print were the names of so many famous American poets, all the way back to Walt Whitman, Emily Dickinson, Ezra Pound, Carl Sandberg, e. e. cummings.

There were others I had met personally: my deceased friend d. a. levy, Allen Ginsberg, Tuli Kupferberg and Clarence Major. The *Writing on the Wall* was in eight sections. My poem was the title poem of a section of mostly unknown poets, except for Gregory Corso and Douglas Blazek.

It was three years since I'd written the poem and read it at The Gate in Cleveland. It horrified me now and I wondered how it had been chosen. Karl Shapiro had been right when he told me about regretting stuff you've already published. I dismissed it as a fluke, a complete accident that bore no relationship to ability as a writer. I didn't need further proof and wasn't going to embarrass myself by writing any more poetry. There were better poets than me everywhere. I didn't show the book to anybody.

I was as hard on myself as my mom would have been. And yet, Ginsberg's poem ended with a muddled, unintelligible line, "Magnanimous reaction to signal Peking isolate space Beings!" The last line of mine was at least a lucid declaration: "We are the war babies."[3]

I made pilgrimages to City Lights Bookstore at the junction of North Beach and Chinatown, but realized I wasn't interested in words. My experiences taking acid hadn't encouraged language and speech and now I was too incoherent to start writing again. Words were a tangle of illusion that ensnared the willing and gullible.

I lost sight of writing things that would be required reading by high school and college students in the future, completely forgot about becoming another Walt Whitman or Carl Sandberg. As a poet I could hope to be no more than a charlatan hobbling shoeless in thrift-store costume upon the world stage, declared an imbecile long ago. I saw that all my careful labor over wit and wordsmithing would end up as so many scraps of paper bundled together in a fragile carton, as insightful as bits of trash found blowing in the wind. Meanwhile popular poets Shel Silverstein and Rod McKuen were cashing in.

I fled Haight-Ashbury to hole up in the derelict Mission District, settling into the same green three-story Victorian apartment building where my New York friend David now lived. The wooden building creaked and rocked with frequent quivers and seismic waves, a flimsy hull afloat on a tectonic landmass that could turn shaky at any time as it nudged its way up the San Andreas Fault. On the top floor I had an aerial lair where I hid from America's frenzy. It was more cheery and spacious than my gloomy garret in Lincoln or my flat in New York had been. Plaster cherub faces from a calmer era adorned the bay window overlooking South Van Ness. Embossed tin wainscoting paneled the private stairway. The vintage kitchen stove was wood-burning on the left and gas on the right.

There were two flats on each level. As units became vacant, more immigrants we had known back east settled in: Valerie from Staten Island, Nick the onetime pay phone saboteur I had met on my first visit to Chicago, David's erstwhile storefront roommate Danny, and Michael, also from Chicago, whom I'd met in New York. I was the only native Californian in the bunch. Eventually we occupied the entire building, along with a parade of temporary roommates, visitors, lovers, and cats and dogs adding to the total population. It took on the communal living atmosphere of Lloyd's East Village apartment. I was the exception, keeping no form of companion and living like an exile. In the general group grope I continued a lonely solitaire in my penthouse. Now and then Darlene phoned me from New York to keep in touch and reminisce. We were still two Nebraska refugees speaking through the lines strung across that same flyover country we'd fled, connected by our common past.

In the afternoons I gathered with the others on the high and wide front stairs above the sidewalk to drink cold beer and watch traffic rushing by on South Van Ness, our version of Siddhartha's timeless river. For income we sometimes bought stacks of the *Berkeley Barb* at wholesale and sold them to tourists near the topless clubs on Broadway, or to afternoon commuters at the train station on Townsend. Some of my friends subsisted on food stamps but I couldn't humiliate myself enough to take a government handout.

I came home one afternoon to fire trucks on the street and everyone from our building huddled on the sidewalk. The abandoned building next door was burning. We thought the fire was caused by a squatter who sometimes camped inside and most likely left a candle burning. Part of the upper flat adjacent to mine also burned, and when the owner made half-hearted repairs we invited city inspectors to come and look. They found so many code violations beyond the fire damage that the building owner unloaded the property on an unsuspecting investor. When no more repairs were forthcoming we went on a rent strike that lasted five years. The *San Francisco Chronicle* wrote a story about us in their Sunday magazine.

Living rent-free in a San Francisco Victorian should have been a sweet setup. For somebody with low expectations, maybe it was. I was nagged by memories from another lifetime, where a junior-high-school counselor told me I was future MIT material. Now when I could have been in graduate school, I was exhausted from travel and bored with the temporary thrill of consciousness-altering chemicals. Thanks to the Vietnam debacle, my extended walkabout on a road less taken had brought me where no college courses and seminars could reach, through an unauthorized piece of untelevised American history. But lately, I wasn't doing much of anything except watching days go by and contemplating the ocean fog that rolled in and spilled over Twin Peaks in the afternoons.

Dropping out wasn't as simple as smoking pot and listening to records, or hitchhiking some place different. It didn't mean renouncing the establishment and joining a so-called counterculture. In some sense, I had been deceived by the yin and the yang. That well-known two-dimensional black and white image conceals a shaman's third realm on its reverse surface. I had been seeking that flip side all along without realizing it. It required leaving the system entirely, going to the heart of understanding, or what some might call a seeker's inward journey.

CHAPTER 30

Three nights a week I crossed the Bay Bridge in a used Volkswagen to labor at a part-time job in Oakland. Athens Bakery was a noisy place of heat and metal. The mixers, conveyors, the oven, the slicing and wrapping machines all were antiquated, dented, patches of bare metal where original paint had worn away. The machinery set the pace and we hustled to keep up. It was demanding physical labor, and many new guys quit after a day or two. I would have too, if I thought I had any other choice. When our work was done, somewhere between midnight and dawn, we'd lock up and I'd drive home covered in dried sweat and white flour. It wasn't a real bakery so much as a factory that made nothing more than burger and hot dog buns for fast food places. "A Better Bun" was the slogan on the side of their orange and white delivery vans. At least it was less boring than sorting mail, and only twenty hours a week on average. At union-scale pay it was enough for me to get by on.

The bakery job left me time on other nights to attend free classes at the city college in the evening. I took a variety of subjects, including astronomy, and soon enrolled as a full-time student during the day, much older than my classmates. The matter of stars had raised so many questions that I signed up for math and physics. Maybe I should have studied poetry.

In bed one night I laid awake and thought about quantum particles. The idea of molecules as empty lattices connecting atoms was nothing new, nor that atoms themselves were merely a few sub-particles zipping around. The astonishing part was that those atomic components weren't three-dimensional solids either. They were tiny wavelets of energy. It followed that the entire physical world had to consist of energy moving through emptiness.

My very own carcass could not be any different. Since early childhood I'd wondered what imprisoned me inside a container-like form. Who was this isolated observer always thinking but always separated from the thoughts of all the world's other observers? According to quantum physics, the sense of a separate physical self had to be an illusion.

Allen Ginsberg had not been so abstract as it sounded, that time he said to me, "You shake hands with a cloud." I too was a cloud of energy wavelets with enormous gaps of vacant space between them. If I looked into the spatial separations between wave-particles, no actual barrier separated the emptiness within my body's molecules from the same emptiness in molecules outside my body. Where did one emptiness end and the other begin?

I laid in the dark and pondered those questions, when I began to notice a melting sensation at the top of my head. Something like the self that lived inside me seemed to be leaking up through my scalp. While my body and the bed and the blankets were left piled in a seamless lump of molecules, the rest of me began seeping through the gaps of my less-than-substantial form, drifting upwards like rising smoke and dispersing into the surrounding ether. I thought I'd ride with it, to see where it took me.

Up near where the ceiling would normally be, I floated as if on my back in a swimming pool, while my physical self remained at the pool's bottom. It wasn't the same as out-of-body experiences are usually described. I didn't actually look down and see my body or go on a ghostly ramble. I didn't begin sailing above roofs and treetops.

There was little time to adjust. In an instant I was no longer a distinct and separate "me" floating in a room with a ceiling and a floor of any kind. I wasn't a separate physical self and I wasn't an isolated observer separated from the thoughts of all the world's other observers. I lost all sense of finite being.

I felt absorbed within a non-divisible multitude, a larger collective mind both generated by and generating our entire universe. The forms of stars and galaxies appeared as white lights in darkness, the way we've always pictured them. The difference was that they weren't "out there." They were "in here" existing within "us." However, inside and outside didn't have the same meaning as they do when you talk about being inside or outside a house. Instead of observed and observer as two separate things, they were now blended into one.

Time seemed to come to a stop, its engine idling. I wondered if I was dead and in the Bardo. Instead of freaking me out though, it was peaceful and reassuring. I considered remaining in that unbound-aried state, detached from my previous identity. On the other hand, it seemed that a specific incarnation had been left behind somewhere. It was the assignment I'd been given, to be a small creature advancing over the planet's terrain, sort of like trekking across Nebraska. Perma-nently abandoning my post wasn't my decision to make. I'd been allowed a privileged glimpse, but now I had an obligation to go back.

I visualized my former body, not as a lattice of molecules and gaps, but as a container again. By channeling my focus enough to locate my left hand, I twitched a finger, which tiny movement reeled me back into my familiar shape, like slipping into a jacket. The whole journey lasted a few minutes at most. I laid on my bed once more, perplexed and caught off guard.

It was like I'd fallen through a looking glass. I'd heard of acid flash-backs but never experienced one. Stoned or not, I'd never hallucinated in the manner of seeing a mirage or apparition or something that wasn't there. Space warps and time portals might be reasonable explanations in the movies, but not to people I knew. I wondered if it had been what they called ego loss.

I confided in my friend at the bakery about my little excursion. He could be insightful at times and I hoped that he would have some helpful observation. This time he was unimpressed and matter-of-fact. He said I had fallen asleep and dreamed. It felt demeaning to be told that, but I didn't blame him. There was no way to prove otherwise, so I decided not to debate with him. I couldn't expect to be believed, any more than I'd ask to be believed if I saw UFOs and aliens. After that I didn't mention it to anyone else, knowing I'd be called delusional, or worse, ridiculed.

I recalled the poem I'd written in high school, the one about the shaman who'd looked into the abyss and never told a soul.

> The pity of the world
> Is that the thoughts of an illiterate poet
> Must go the way
>   Of smoke and shade...

Drifting entirely away from my body and blending with all consciousness and matter didn't happen again. I began to grow suspicious about having been privy to the entire universe simultaneously seeing and being itself. I was even now still isolated and separated from the thoughts of all the world's other occupants. At times though, I would notice myself spontaneously slipping into the emptiness between quantum particles. Mundane activities of living felt like a horror movie where part of me had not returned to Earth. I felt as insubstantial as a neutrino slicing through this world without altering it or forming attachment.

I experienced something like the observer effect in quantum physics, where watching my own actions interfered with my intended actions. It made for an awkward performance when I tried to function in a world once taken for granted. Then I learned that western psychology had another name for it: depersonalization/derealization disorder. In our material culture, built upon and geared to tangibles, DPDR was viewed as a disfunction instead of an ability. I wished I lived in a Himalayan country where intangible reality was gravely acknowledged.

I felt like the lone escapee from Plato's allegorical cave, the one who left and saw the sun. When he came back to tell others that there was more out there than the shadows they were used to looking at, they rejected his announcement. I wouldn't be so foolish. There was that cryptic line in the *Tao Te Ching* about "Those who know don't tell." It wasn't so much that those who know weren't willing to tell, as that without a better language for it they weren't able to tell their tale without sounding absurd. To write the things they did, I thought some of those ancients like Plato and Lao Tzu must have had experiences similar to mine.

With or without a suitable interpretation, I found that the end effect on me was the same. Monitoring my appearance and public behavior took some careful effort. I caught myself being an imposter of myself, as if acting in a stage play, at times only pretending to be me. I attempted to behave like a primate, exactly like the 13th Floor Elevators sang about, living on Monkey Island and trying to be a monkey too. I was an unauthorized visitor. When no one seemed to suspect me in their midst, I puppeteered my puppet body onward, casting shadows that I hoped others thought were believable. How I'd fare incognito, undercover in the native population, like a complete unknown, remained uncertain.

In the meantime, an endless roving poker game took place in some of the apartments downstairs. No real money changed hands because we could only afford to play for pennies and nickels. Enough weed circulated to keep it all on the surrealistic side. Some of the players seemed genuinely amused most of the time, but I was not entertained by the repetitive games, nor engaged by the trivial stakes. I was mostly at the table to endure the mortal hours.

We gathered together through the long nights, between the garish light of an exposed bulb overhead and the wide planks beneath our boots, nailed down by Victorian carpenters who built houses the way they once built ships. We sailed as on a fragile barque through the night that pressed against the outside walls like a sea. We were rushing down a churning and bucking whitewater current that no vessel had ever been known to survive. Not so much sailors as tidal wave survivors clinging to flotsam, we focused on our cards and waited out the long hours after midnight, drinking red wine, dark ale, and rye whiskey, until we were indifferent to the knowledge that our ship could go under at any moment.

ENDNOTES

Chapter 2

1. Steve Clay Wilson (1941-2021). In a couple of years S. Clay Wilson would be one of San Francisco's notorious underground artists. His cartoons, featuring the Checkered Demon and Star-Eyed Stella, appeared in *ZAP Comix*.

2. Steve Abbott (1943-1992) became the editor of *Poetry Flash* in San Francisco in the early eighties, a gay rights activist, and much later the subject of *Fairyland: A Memoir of My Father* written by his daughter Alysia Abbott. But for now he was simply my friend Steve Abbott.

3. Carl Davidson (b. 1943) was national vice-president of SDS in 1966-7, an associate of Tom Hayden, Carl Oglesby, and Bill Ayers. In his book *Armies of the Night*, Norman Mailer wrote about seeing Davidson at the 1967 march on the Pentagon.

Chapter 5

1. Clarence Major (b. 1936) Professor, University of California, Davis, 1989–2003 and Distinguished Professor, University of California, 2003–2017, was awarded the 26th "Annual PEN Oakland-Reginald Lockett Lifetime Achievement Award 2016" on December 3, 2016.

Chapter 6

1. Darryl Levy, AKA d. a. levy (1942-1968) Legendary Cleveland mimeograph-revolution poet and publisher. Original works preserved in universities, museums, rare book collections.

2. Taylor, Kent and Alan Horvath. "d.a. levy Publications: Bibliography." Internet. http://www.thing.net/~grist/ld/dalevy/lev-b-p.htm. Accessed 3 Oct. 2017.

Chapter 7

1. More than fifty years later copies of *Do-It!* were for sale by online sellers. A copy in Amsterdam could be bought for 200 Euros, in California for $250, in Minneapolis for $500.

2. WorldCat is a union catalog that itemizes the collections of 72,000 libraries in 170 countries and territories that participate in the Online Computer Library Center (OCLC) global cooperative. *Paracutes* OCLC number is 12282378.
3. Later I found out that at that exact time, in June 1966, Ginsberg wrote a poem titled "Cleveland, The Flats" and dedicated it "To D. A. Levy."

Chapter 9

1. Free Love Press. Now listed in WorldCat with OCLC number 3416418. There are four volumes from three readings. Volume 4 is from the third reading on July 1, 1966. Copies of *Poets At the Gate* are held in eight collections.
2. On the internet I found a nostalgic tribute titled "Remembering Adele's." The blog about Cleveland's bar on Euclid Avenue had existed for a few years by the time I discovered it. Its creator, Paul Hilcof, recalled a legion of Adele's regulars and some of the occasionals. I remembered many of them, and to my surprise found an entry about me. "A traveling poet named Randy Rhody breezed through town on his way east from Chicago. I bought him a beer and he gave me a copy of his poetry magazine, "Paracutes." It had a hand-painted cover, on which he inscribed a thank-you note for the beer."

Chapter 10

1. West, Hedy. "500 Miles." Performed by Peter, Paul and Mary. *Peter, Paul and Mary*. Warner Bros., 1962.

Chapter 12

1. A copy of *4 Suits* eventually came to rest in the University of Virginia library special collections as a rare book, with its own WorldCat OCLC number, 22220492. Another copy was offered by an online book seller for thirty-five dollars.
2. In 1973 the *New York Times* printed Edward English's obituary, saying he was about 58 years old. It described him as a vagabond poet and mentioned his unpublished *Nature's Creation* manuscript.
3. McDaniel, Ellas a.k.a. Bo Diddley. "Who Do You Love?" Checker Records, 1956.

Chapter 13

1. Soon Jefferson Airplane, Grateful Dead, Big Brother and the Holding Company, Thirteenth Floor Elevators, Jimi Hendrix, and Vanilla Fudge would all put out records, but *Freak Out!* was ahead of them all.

Chapter 14

1. Cotten, Elizabeth. "Freight Train." Performed by Rusty Draper. Mercury Records, 1957.

Chapter 15

1. Something about the band's two-week show being extended to four weeks but not having hotel rooms for the added two weeks.
2. Ambrose Bierce was a journalist from the *San Francisco Chronicle* in the late 1800s who wrote *The Devil's Dictionary* (e.g., "Admiration: Our polite recognition of another's resemblance to ourselves.") and who disappeared in Mexico in 1914, during the revolution.
3. It was the last time I saw Levy. In the year ahead he and Jim Lowell of Asphodel Book Shop, the local store that carried his works, were harassed by the police for obscenity. Levy's printing equipment was confiscated. Allen Ginsberg went to Cleveland to organize a legal defense fund for him, but I didn't know about any of that.
4. If I could, I'd go back and tell her how much her kindness still reaches me decades later, along with the black guy at Rawlins who gave me lunch money.

Chapter 16

1. Troup, Bobby. "Route 66." Performed by Chuck Berry. Chess Records, 1961.

Chapter 17

1. It was the Love-Pageant Rally of October 6, 1966 and I pretty much missed it.

Chapter 18

1. Wilson, Brian and Love, Mike. "Good Vibrations." Performed by The Beach Boys. October 10, 1966, Capitol Records.

Chapter 19

1. *The Wild Angels*. Released July 20, 1966. American International Pictures.

Chapter 20

1. Almost 400,000 guys like me were drafted that year, half of them sent to Vietnam. Consider that three future American presidents were also draft dodgers at the time.

Chapter 22

1. Later known as Peter Coyote, the actor.
2. "In the Clear." *San Francisco Chronicle*, November 30, 1966. Page 1.
3. The car and two drivers were like a scene from the movie *Two-Lane Blacktop* made five years later in 1971, starring James Taylor, Dennis Wilson, and Warren Oates. We were on the same stretch of highway as the film.

Chapter 24

1. This was the Bernalillo County jail that Kirk Douglas and the Indians broke out of in *Lonely Are the Brave*.

Chapter 27

1. Randolfe Hayden Wicker (b. Charles Gervin Hayden, Jr., 1938).
2. While researching I found a Portland book dealer offering *Sum*, described as "Soft cover. Book Condition: Very Good. Lakewood: sum, 1966. Unpaginated. Stapled wraps. Cover toned at the edges, small stain on front cover. Rare. Cover art by Dagmar." It included work by d. a. levy, Anne McCormick, A. Greenshoot, Kent Taylor, Grace Butcher, Randy Rhody, Dagmar. The seller was asking $120, and five dollars shipping.
3. Walter Lowenfels (1897-1976) American poet.

Chapter 29

1. In time Cleveland State University assembled a d. a. levy collection as part of a Cleveland Memory Project, elevating him to home town hero too late for it to matter.
2. *The Writing on the Wall*, Walter Lowenfels, editor. Hardcover, Doubleday, July 1969. ISBN 0385017448.
3. The unique and paradoxical anti-war term War Babies was quickly replaced in the journalistic mind by Baby Boomer, a label that robbed us of identity and the just causes we stood for.

ABOUT THE AUTHOR

Randy Rhody's poems survive in publications from the mimeograph revolution that found their way into the archives of university libraries and the inventory of booksellers asking rare-book prices.

At thirty-one, Rhody graduated from the University of California at Berkeley with a degree in astronomy. As an engineer at Lockheed Missiles and Space Company he operated on-orbit military satellites and supported space shuttle missions. He lives with his wife in Los Altos, California.

CPSIA information can be obtained
at www.ICGtesting.com
Printed in the USA
BVHW071154071021
618420BV00001B/71